Surviving the Academy
Feminist Perspectives

Edited by

Danusia Malina
and
Sian Maslin-Prothero

UK   Falmer Press, 1 Gunpowder Square, London, EC4A 3DE

USA   Falmer Press, Taylor & Francis Inc., 325 Chestnut Street, 8th Floor, Philadelphia, PA 19106

First published in 1998

A catalogue record for this book is available from the British Library

ISBN 0 7507 0924 3 paper

Library of Congress Cataloging-in-Publication Data are available on request

Jacket design by Caroline Archer

Typeset in 10/12 pt Times by
Graphicraft Limited, Hong Kong

Printed in Great Britain by Biddles Ltd., Guildford and King's Lynn on paper which has a specified pH value on final paper manufacture of not less than 7.5 and is therefore 'acid free'.

Contents

Contents

Foreword

The roots of this volume lie in the 1996 Women in Higher Education Network (WHEN) conference. Why, about a century after women first fought for entry to higher education, is it still necessary for women to 'speak our place(s)'?

In the case of the student population overall, the situation looks quite good numerically. The proportion of women UK undergraduates is roughly equivalent to the proportion of women in the population as a whole. However, women students are still under-represented in the physical science and engineering disciplines, and for the majority on education and language courses. Thus there is a considerable gender divide, with women students still concentrated in what have been considered traditionally 'female' subject areas (Department for Education, 1994; Universities Statistical Record, 1994).

The situation for those who teach these women students is unsatisfactory. In no disciplinary areas do the number of women academic staff outnumber those of men, even in those areas where women form the majority of students. Moreover, the distribution of women academics across the hierarchy of grades is remarkably skewed; women form the vast majority of contract researchers and a small minority of senior lecturers and professors. Overall, where institutional and managerial academic power is, women are not. Where employment is insecure, low status and poorly paid, women are.

When it comes to difference between women academics, it is difficult for us to say much about the combined effects of gender, ethnicity and class. While statistics are now collected on students' ethnic origins, there are no official figures on the number of black women academics. And while we supposedly know about students' class backgrounds from statistics collected on their (mainly) fathers' occupations, once women get an academic post they automatically become classified as middle-class, even though from autobiographical accounts we know they do not feel it (Mahoney and Zmroczek, 1997; Walkerdine and Lucey, 1989). Questions of sexuality and disability, as well as the place of non-academic women in the higher education system, such as domestic and clerical workers, are also major silences in official statistics.

Unless we adopt a purely liberal equal opportunities agenda, however, we have to ask what difference it would make if the diversity of women were equally represented in all disciplinary areas and across the academic hierarchy? The entry of women as numerical individuals onto the higher education scene does not necessarily shift the academic knowledge-making project, or the exercise of academic power, as masculinist-defined activities.

There is now a relatively considerable body of feminist work that has unpacked the assumptions behind traditional academic knowledge-making (including, Aptheker,

1989; Belenkey et al., 1986; Rose, 1994; Smith, 1987; Spender, 1981). A boundary has been supposedly objective, detached and neutral academic ways of knowing (characteristically posed as masculine attributes) and detailed, subjective and emotional ways of knowing (characteristically posed as feminine attributes). Some feminist thinkers have worked towards an integration of the two ways of knowing theoretically (including those referenced above). They have melded subjectivity and objectivity, love and science, dailyness and generality, self and others, and process and effect, in an attempt to break down the patriarchal binaries and hierarchical bases of academic knowledge. Some of these simple attempts have been inspired by investigations of the experiences of women as students in higher education. The impact of such work, though, has been negligible outside feminist circles. This way of reconceptualizing the knowledge-making process seems to be both a personal and political threat to those wedded to masculinist thought — amongst whom women can be found.

For those women academics who have broken through the 'glass ceiling' and taken on a managerial role, there is the question of the exercise of academic power. This poses particular problems if they are feminists who wish to work in cooperative and women-friendly ways. Women with power in academia have to exercise it in a culture which has been shaped predominantly by men, and which latterly has been concerned with measuring inputs and outputs, quality assessments, and competition between departments and institutions. Few of the recent developments in higher education are conducive to feminist ways of operating (Morley, 1995; Skeggs, 1995), and feminist academics may find themselves uneasily fluctuating between patriarchal and feminist modes of management.

Thus, questions about women in higher education concern more than how many women are in what positions, as the contributions to this volume demonstrate. The authors discuss a range of issues affecting a diversity of women in higher education — their roles and practices at different levels, in a variety of disciplinary areas — and explore the creation of spaces for dialogue and cooperation.

Ultimately, women and feminism in the academy — as elsewhere — is about finding another starting point for our understandings and theorizing, and our practices. The WHEN conference and this volume provide two of the spaces for a diversity of women to speak their concerns, and to raise questions about their place(s) in higher education.

Rosalind Edwards
Reader in Social Policy
Social Sciences Research Centre
South Bank University

References

APTHEKER, B. (1989) *Tapestries of Life: Women's Work, Women's Consciousness, and the Daily Learning of Experience*, Amhurst: University of Massachusetts Press.

BELENKEY, M.F., CLINCHY, B.M., GOLDBERGER, N.R. and TARULE, J.M. (1986) *Women's Ways of Knowing: The Development of Self, Voice and Mind*, New York: Basic Books.

DEPARTMENT FOR EDUCATION (1994) *Education Statistics for the United Kingdom: 1994 Edition*, London: HMSO.

MAHONEY, P. and ZMROCZEK, C. (1997) *Class Matters: 'Working-Class' Women Discuss Social Class*, London: Taylor and Francis.

MORLEY, L. (1995) 'The micropolitics of women's studies: Feminism and organisational change in the academy', in MAYNARD, M. and PURVIS, J. (eds) *Heterosexual Politics*, London: Taylor and Francis.

ROSE, H. (1994) *Love, Power and Knowledge: Towards a Feminist Transformation of the Sciences*, Cambridge: Polity Press.

SKEGGS, B. (1995) 'Women's studies in Britain in the 1990s: Entitlement cultures and institutional constraints', *Women's Studies International Forum*, **18**, 4, pp. 475–85.

SMITH, D.E. (1987) *The Everyday World as Problematic: A Feminist Sociology*, Boston: North-eastern University.

SPENDER, D. (ed.) (1981) *Men's Studies Modified: The Impact of Feminism on the Academic Disciplines*, Oxford: Pergamon Press.

UNIVERSITIES STATISTICAL RECORD (1994) *University Statistics 1993–1994*, Vol. 1, Cheltenham: USR.

WALKERDINE, V. and LUCEY, H. (1989) *Democracy in the Kitchen: Regulating Mothers and Socialising Daughters*, London: Virago.

Introduction

Danusia Malina and Sian Maslin-Prothero

This collection arises from the Women in Higher Education Network (WHEN) UK 1996 conference, organized by the University of Central Lancashire. This edited collection also marks a new series and commitment to feminist publishing by Taylor and Francis book publishers. Among the aims of the new series is to: '. . . integrate theory and experience; demonstrate women's creativity in what are still hostile environments; and contribute to the development of interdisciplinary feminist awareness, theory and dialogue . . .' (Walsh, 1996, p. 1). The book builds on Louise Morley and Val Walsh's 1996 book, as they identify: 'Breaking boundaries involves naming barriers to women's participation in higher education, as well as testifying to the consequences of power relations based on social class, "race", sexuality, age, disabilities, and ethnicities' (1996, p. 34). This collection highlights some underexposed areas of concern for women in higher education, identifying the organizational and institutional masculinities that persist in the academy.

Those presenting conference papers and workshops in 1996 were invited to submit papers for review by the book editors. From over 70 papers, nine papers were chosen for inclusion in the book. However, there were some obvious gaps including friendship, disability and black women, therefore we as editors, commissioned additional chapters.

It is important not to lose sight of the difference between the conference and the book. The conference provided presenters with space to give papers or experiential workshops and test out their ideas. The leap from conference paper to book chapter is enormous. The material presented at the conference is changed and adapted to 'fit' the academic framework of a scholarly volume. As editors, we were torn between 'retaining' the author's own voice and making their contribution fit the shape of the book, as well as ensuring their chapters as being seen as academically acceptable and valuable in the eyes of our reviewers and readers of this collection. The editorial process has not been an easy one, we wanted to nurture new talent as well as utilize established writers. Achieving this balance has been challenging. As Dale Spender says '. . . we simply cannot afford to hit so hard at our sisters so that they withdraw and determine not to risk themselves again' (Spender, 1985, p. 211).

Our aim in assembling this collection has been to draw out the public/private divide. As women we are pulled in different directions; we are women; we also have 'familial' responsibilities, encompassing a variety of different forms, as sisters, mothers, carers and lovers. Finally, we are also workers, in the public domain, where our relationships with co-workers places us in another locality. This makes our lives complex as we move from one context to another, changing the way we present ourselves accordingly. This adapting and changing leads us to feeling a sense of vulnerability and insecurity. How do you retain a radical edge in your work, when your child is ill (see Carol Munn-Giddings, Chapter 5) or when you have concerns about being tokenistic (see Chapter 13)? The book falls into three sections each of which explores the intricate relationships between women, their lives and higher education. These different roles and relationships continue to create tensions in our personal and professional lives, as Rosalind Edwards says: '. . . the public/private dichotomy still operates.' (1993, p. 23); these tensions and the continued sexual division of labour in the workplace are explored throughout the book. And yet women have diverse strategies for surviving in the academy.

Section 1: Power: Challenging 'Care' in Higher Education

In the first section issues around power and care in higher education are examined. This includes a variety of perspectives; from the relationship between lecturers, students and pastoral care; through to a professor of social work exploring the perceived powerlessness of social work in the academy, in relation to other disciplines. Of women breaking out and free from the boundaries (Morley and Walsh, 1996) and stereotypes associated with us, only to find we are knee deep in treacle and still finding it difficult to move.

This section starts with Pamela Cotterill and Ruth Waterhouse's chapter which explores the way in which the move towards mass higher education has significantly changed the tutor's pastoral role and the nature of the student/staff relationship. Drawing on the authors' experience as women's studies tutors, they examine what they see as the gap between the corporate rhetoric and the reality of both student and staff experience. Despite the importance placed on the quality of the student experience by the Higher Education Funding Council, they suggest that a devaluing of both pastoral support and the enabling role of the tutor has occurred. They argue that the emotional labour within higher education has much more in common with many forms of feminized work, especially its invisibility and low status. Comparisons are drawn with debates surrounding community care policy with particular focus on the issues of resourcing and cost efficiency. Emphasis is also placed on the conflicts between the feminist philosophies underpinning women's studies courses and institutional demands on staff concerning teaching commitments, research and administration. They raise questions about the tensions between the 'open access' approach in mass higher education and the diversity of student need which this will inevitably produce.

LesleyAnne Ezelle and Lindsay Hill explore the central premise that sexuality and sexual identity, as theory and lived experience, span across the human sciences. The workshops aim to provide all students with the opportunity to explore their experiences and to acquire a body of knowledge that would inform both their personal and professional lives. However, the authors argue that there is an absence of discourse which acknowledges and celebrates diversity; and that the body of knowledge which informs vocational training is based upon theories and principles of patriarchal heterosexuality. This has a negative impact upon lesbians, bisexual and heterosexual women in their roles as either students or teachers. This chapter examines, from a feminist perspective, some of the problems and barriers to teaching sexuality and sexual identity in health and social work training which involves challenging patriarchal heterosexuality whilst exploring the implications for lesbian, bisexual and heterosexual women. To conceptualize the process of change, the authors have used the earthquake/firm ground model to discuss the problems and make recommendations. Sally French describes the barriers to full inclusion experienced by a visually impaired lecturer in higher education. The discussion is set within the context of the employment situation of visually disabled people in the UK today. The barriers experienced are explored by reference to the social model of disability where disability is explained, not in terms of impairment, but in terms of social, structural and environmental barriers. The chapter concludes by considering whether equal opportunities policies have had any effect on the lives of visually disabled people working in higher education.

This section ends with Lena Dominelli's exploration of women in social work education who have a particular experience of gender shaped by their position *vis-à-vis* male academics and the particularities of social work as a women's profession. Social work's position in the academy is precarious and becoming even more so. This chapter traces the implications of this reality for women academics and the discipline in a context in which the educational agenda is being redefined by the emphasis on more expensive research projects to the detriment of teaching and student care. To survive in this highly problematic environment, women social work educators need to form alliances with colleagues across the university setting and students. Thus, to make the academy a more congenial place for women to receive recognition for their work, develop their creative potential and propose more humanistic forms of education, women need to become involved in transforming social relations across the board.

Section 2: Maternalism in the Academy

In the second section maternalism in the academy is considered. The assumption in higher education is that because you are a woman you care, you do not have to have parental responsibilities to bring these attributes to your work environment. Carol Munn-Giddings starts this section by exploring how the experience of motherhood articulates with and is currently in conflict with the role of an 'academic' in higher education institutions. The structural, organizational and cultural value base of academia effectively works to the detriment of academics with caring responsibilities. The literature that does exist reflects an inverse relationship between caring responsibilities for children and academic success, moreover this relationship is gendered. It is women with childcare responsibilities that are losing out. Interrelated with the existing literature in this area examples from the authors and others' experiences highlight and illustrate the tensions that are created by the academy but played out between staff members. The research and literature in this area is scarce. The chapter concludes by arguing for the importance of feminist research in this area and in doing so indicates some of the tensions between motherhood and feminism which play a large part in accounting for the paucity of interest in this area.

Tina Barnes-Powell and Gayle Letherby move the maternalism debate forward with an examination of the gendered nature of 'care work' within higher education. The chapter examines the experience of two female academics in a new university. Firstly, the authors discuss the range of 'care work' that they became involved in during the course of an academic year. Secondly, they set their experiences into a broader debate which addresses more general issues of power and responsibility within higher education. Their chapter illustrates how women are expected to care for and about students, in comparison to men; the assumption is that women care and are maternal.

Sandra Wilkins develops this theme further by discussing clerical work in the academy. Gender segregation and the process of feminization of the workforce have been examined, and identification of a class structure has been the focus of a number of studies. Recent technological developments and changes in organizational structures have transformed work patterns. Whilst deskilling or downgrading of skills have been the predicted outcome of these changes, recent empirical evidence suggests that, for secretaries, widespread reskilling and acquisition of new skills has occurred. Within higher education administration reduction in routine typing following the widespread use of word processors by all staff has significantly changed work patterns. A shift in emphasis from 'working for' to 'working with' has enabled secretaries to assume many administrative tasks formerly undertaken by academics. This has obvious benefits, but the failure to recognize increased responsibilities, together with the lack of structured career pathways remains a problem. The influence of gender and class in perpetuating stereotypical assumptions about the role of secretaries is of key concern. This chapter highlights the importance that value, recognition and respect have in authenticating new identities relating to the contemporary secretarial role.

Robyn Thomas concludes this section with her chapter which examines women academics' experiences of the gendered university culture, during a period of rapid change in higher education. The new discourses of human resource management in higher education have been promoted through a range of disciplinary technologies, including the introduction of academic appraisal. From a Foucauldian perspective, the functioning of appraisal can be seen to be reshaping the nature of academic work, controlling behaviour, changing expectations and challenging professional identities. The research, upon which this chapter is based, explores how individual subjectivity, the academic profession and university cultures are defined and contested through the new management discourses. The chapter explores women academics' responses to the new gender culture of the academy.

Section 3: Collective Action: Standing Still or Moving Forward?

The final section of the book draws on a range of different, positive experiences. Avril Butler's chapter is a reflective account of the setting up of a feminist research group within an English university and explores some of the issues that this has raised. The context for the work is one of increasing demands on women academics to produce research publications without acknowledgment of the obstacles to women which are embedded in the well established male-dominated structures. The group is multi-disciplinary and includes women with a variety of connections to the university. The group has evolved a form of meeting which offers space to each woman's work and an atmosphere of supportive criticism. The chapter includes some commentary on what these processes are, how they have created them and reflections on the difficulties and conflicts and how they have been dealt with. The aim of the chapter is to stimulate discussion of the issues involved in creating an alternative space within an institution, the benefits it brings and the danger of reproducing exclusive dynamics.

Ann Kettle's chapter is a discussion, based on personal experience, of the role of the trade union in collective action by women employed in higher education in the late 1990s. Issues involving women which require collective action are identified and examined by reference to the author's 30 years' experience as a university teacher and 10 years' experience as an activist in the Association of University Teachers locally and nationally. There follows a tentative exploration of the tensions involved in collective action and trade union activism, such as the difficulty of speaking for women academics as a whole, 'the re-inventing the wheel' syndrome, union resistance to the privileging of women's issues and the problems posed by such contentious matters as sexual harassment and consensual relationships between staff and students. The aim is to establish that, as far as women working in higher education are concerned, the personal is still the political and that, in spite of the tensions involved, collective action is still required and that women have a significant role to play in trade unions, both nationally and in their own institutions.

Sonia Thompson's chapter identifies her experience of being a black woman in the academy. There follows an exploration of the difference between black and white women in higher education, particularly in relationship to the unequal power relationships that exist between them. The chapter emphasizes the importance of acknowledging the complexity of black women's situation in relation to class, sex and race. In order to survive and thrive in higher education black women need to forge alliances with other black women. However, whether true friendship can exist between black women and white women is another question. Bridges need to be built, but on something stronger than a shared victimization, white women need to make the move if these alliances are to work.

Gabriele Griffin argues that following the expansion of women's studies in the UK during the 1980s, the 1990s have witnessed rising uncertainty about the nature and status of women's studies within higher education, expressed through the lack of jobs and departments with the title 'Women's studies' in the UK as well as through the absence of the category women's studies in the research assessment exercise and similar publicly driven exercises. The consequent precarious position of women's studies in the academy has in part been promoted further by general changes in higher education in the UK, such as modularization and restructuring which, while potentially useful to multi- and inter-disciplinary subjects, have not proved so because macro structures in institutions have failed to adjust to accommodate the implications of these changes. Women's studies as a discipline itself has matured, with increasing numbers of students graduating with first degrees in the subject. The chapter suggests that strategically working to secure the discipline includes a review of the kinds of courses we offer, collaborations around research and through that the development of much larger departments or schools of women's studies.

Finally, Danusia Malina and Sian Maslin-Prothero examine another form of collective action, that is of publishing. This final chapter openly debates the process of feminist editing and explores the ways women, in a competitive environment, can reproduce male agendas. Women have set-up their own systems of publishing including journals and feminist series publications. This book is a first in a new series for Taylor and Francis, demonstrating their continued commitment to feminist perspectives. In addition, women have continued to develop their publication record in mainstream journals. However, there are still areas where women need to break out and be speaking their places.

References

EDWARDS, R. (1993) *Mature Women Students: Separating or Connecting Family and Education*, London: Taylor and Francis.

MORLEY, L. and WALSH, V. (eds) (1996) *Breaking Boundaries: Women in Higher Education*, London: Taylor and Francis.

SPENDER, D. (1985) *For the Record: The Making and Meaning of Feminist Knowledge*, London: The Women's Press.

WALSH, V. (1996) Personal communication.

Section 1

Power: Challenging Care in Higher Education

1   Women in Higher Education: The Gap between Corporate Rhetoric and the Reality of Experience

Pamela Cotterill and Ruth L. Waterhouse

Introduction

We are two lecturers working in the field of women's studies. Our background and training is in the discipline of sociology but our expertise has become increasingly diversified since our engagement with women's studies. Several years ago we presented a paper at the Women's Studies Network (UK) Conference. At that time we were very new to the issues raised by attempting to teach women's studies within the context of mass higher education. Struggling with the complex and combined processes of modularization, semesterization and rationalization, we approached our task of establishing a half degree and 'Masters' (sic) with some degree of trepidation. Our paper for that particular conference was called 'Women's studies: Feminist dream or feminist nightmare?'. In retrospect, our experience has shown that women's studies teaching can indeed fulfil our feminist dreams but the context in which we attempt to work with students has increasingly proven to be a nightmare. Whilst we wrote the first paper in a half finished office, in the midst of what seemed like a perpetual building site (mass education expansion), we are writing this second paper in the context of Teaching Quality Assessment evaluation and the demands placed upon us by the forthcoming Research Assessment Exercise. We feel ourselves somewhat under siege from the competing and frequently contradictory demands of teaching, pastoral care, research and administration.

As we write, a queue of anxious students is beginning to form outside our door. It is the deadline for student assignments. It is the time for extensions to be negotiated. A stressful time for both staff and students as we all attempt (and fail) to meet our own particular deadlines. Life beyond the so-called academy is put on hold until the pressure eases up. But the longed for cessation of pressure does not happen. Staff and students alike complain of 'burn out', mysterious and unidentifiable physical complaints and soured personal relationships (Fisher, 1994).

As we ply our trade at the computer we know we do so at the cost of not hearing out the student who needs an extension because a) her mother has died; b) her partner has destroyed her work; c) she is coming to terms with the aftermath of a violent sexual assault.

Setting the Scene

Those of us who work in the so-called 'new universities' have always been more familiar with concrete blocks than ivory towers. Building expansion on every available green space means that ours is rapidly resembling a gigantic Pizza Hut. Perhaps this is intentional given the rationalization of higher education in recent years. The drive towards open access, increased student numbers (Cowell, 1996), modularity and credit transfers suggests that all institutions should be doing the same thing in the same way. Ritzer (1993) has called this the 'McDonaldization' of higher education, where institutions of learning can be compared with every city centre shopping mall and fast food outlet.

Changes in higher education since 1992 have affected all of us who work within it. Higher education is now characterized by greater managerial power, tighter hierarchical structures and limited involvement in the decision-making process for those below senior management level. Within this context teaching, administration and research are subject to internal and external scrutiny for quality performance. Internally, these include performance-related pay and promotion opportunities, whilst external measures are imposed by central government through Teaching Quality Assessment and Research Assessment Exercise. The result is greater competition between colleagues in the drive to publish, increased teaching and administrative loads and less personalized involvement with students. However, these demands are not evenly spread among academics. Those who are 'successful' researchers (success measured by an ability to attract external funding and an output which merits inclusion in the Research Assessment Exercise) are able to negotiate different working conditions than 'less productive' colleagues. (Cooper, 1996; Richards, 1996) This means reduced teaching and administrative responsibilities for them but increased loads for others. The result, within a context where greatest value is placed on research as an academic endeavour, is major changes in the way academics view themselves and are viewed.

The development of a management culture has been underpinned by corporate rhetoric expressed in 'strategic plans' and 'mission statements'. These have become an important part of the marketing of higher education as well as serving to justify the role of management in planning and decision-making. National policy on expanding access to higher education is committed to providing access for all students with the ability to benefit. Certain areas have been identified in which special initiatives will be developed. This will involve increasing the number of applications from specific student groups. In particular, these include mature students, students from ethnic minorities, students with disabilities and women students.

Many people, ourselves among them, recognize the benefits of a heterogeneous student community. Therefore, a policy which seeks to break down barriers to university entrance and actively welcomes diversity is one which we would support. However, once access to higher education is achieved, heterogeneity gives way to homogeneity in that the ability to benefit from higher education seems, increasingly, to lie squarely on the shoulders of the students. In other words, diversity is valued only as far as students' lived experiences outside the university do not impact on their lives as students within the university in problematic ways.

As the numbers of students entering higher education rapidly increased in the early 1990s, the corridors seemed to resound with a collective distress born of student poverty, debt, ill health and personal problems. (Saunders, 1995; Fisher, 1994). Yet as women's studies tutors we were bound, at one level of analysis, to welcome attempts to bring students into the university system. Like our counterparts in the mental health system, we were only too aware of the wastage, inequities and injustices of the established system. As people interested in human rights generally and women's rights in particular, we had to be in favour of the rhetoric of mass higher education and care in the community. So as those involved in institutionalized care of the sick and elderly ushered their 'clients' *out* into the community, we welcomed our 'clients' *into* the institutions of higher learning. For as they say, when 'one door closes another door opens!'. But the communities these two 'client' groups were encouraged to embrace were not always welcoming or, indeed, safe spaces. For many they have proved to be both destructive and hostile to their interests. For the recipients of care in the community, the personal costs have sometimes been high and the care provision woefully low (Morris, 1993; Walker, 1993.) Likewise, the recipients of mass higher education have often been treated to what is known in the official jargon as 'student led/student centred' learning; colloquially known as the 'fuck off and find out' model of education. Invited to the banquet of education, they have subsequently been told to stand in line at the cafeteria check out queue of the modular system. That university architecture increasingly emulates the 'fast food' eating houses should come as no surprise. The education received there is equally fast and sometimes just as unhealthy and difficult to digest.

Mass higher education was in part predicated on the assumption that women students, particularly mature women students, would exploit the expanded opportunities to study. Yet these are the very people who were expected to take up the responsibilities and duties inherent in community care policies. The double burden of women's work was to be further complicated by additional caring duties and the pressures to 'get an education'. Education, like paid work, is constructed as secondary to women's domestic responsibilities. However, university education, like employment outside the home, reduces women's availability to act as carers of dependent children and adults. Yet community care policy is founded on the assumption that women are not only available but *willing* to care. The notion of women's 'natural' caring abilities has been well documented (Finch and Groves, 1983; Ungerson, 1987; Lewis and Meredith, 1988; Qureshi and Walker, 1989) and the rhetoric of 'informal care' in social policy barely attempts to disguise assumptions that this can and should be undertaken by women for free. For example, the Griffiths Report (1988) asserts that public services should 'take account of how best to support and maintain the role of the informal carer' (p. 7) yet does not 'recommend any extension of social service authorities' limited powers to make cash payments to individuals' (p. 14). A potential challenge to informal patterns of care comes from higher education targets to increase the numbers of mature and women students. However, the growing trend in women's participation in the labour market has not corresponded with a noticeable decline in caring responsibilities (Qureshi and Walker, 1989) and there is no evidence to suggest that women entering higher education will prioritize study over care. What is emerging is evidence of conflict between the two, resulting in physical and emotional strain for students attempting to carry out both.

Similarly, the lack of public childcare provision clearly reflects the assumption that care of dependent children is a private matter. Furthermore, the rhetoric of 'shared parenting' does not obscure the fact that it is mothers who are the main carers of dependent children and it is they who must organize alternative childcare arrangements when undertaking paid work or entering higher education. Women-friendly timetables designed to fit in and around school hours will soon be a thing of the past as universities move towards a 12-hour teaching day. Government response to an increasing need for parental support has been one of non-intervention taking the view that childcare is not a public issue. This means that childcare is left to the vagaries of the market where it is assumed that private enterprise will respond to women's needs, or informal support through the mother's family and friendship networks (Brannen and Moss, 1991; Cotterill, 1992).

Set these demands on women's physical and emotional energy against the realities of the declining value of student grants and the abolition of housing benefit and mature student allowances and a nightmare scenario does, indeed, begin to present itself. Those who inhabit the nightmare are outside our office door as we continue to write.

"Lady, What Do You Do All Day?"

Contrary to popular mythology, being a student in higher education has never been easy yet the mythology persists. Only a few weeks ago one of us was subjected to the apocryphal belief that all students are 'wealthy, lazy, privileged and "high" most of the time on drugs'. The reality is, of course, very different. For many students, particularly mature women, 'leisure is just a mythology'. Many women's studies students have much in common with folk singer Peggy Seeger's housewife who protests:

I'm a production line all by myself, only my wages are missing . . . (Seeger, 1992)

Her song encapsulates and articulates the competing demands placed upon contemporary women. Seeger's lyrics address the difficulties of perpetually balancing unpaid domestic work and paid work. Many women's studies students, thanks to the effects of 'care in the community' programs, also have to care for sick and/or older relatives. As Peggy Seeger sings with heavy irony:

I care for a lovely old mother-in-law, She's 87 and cranky. (Seeger, 1992)

11

It seems to us that corporate rhetoric about 'open access' to higher education ignores the conflicts which students experience between the domestic side and university side of their lives. The demands of home, childcare and care of adults conflict with the demands of university timetables, attendance at lectures and seminars and assignment deadlines. Negotiating the boundaries between the public and private spheres and meeting the demands of both is difficult for increasing numbers of women students. Their primary identification is with the private world and often domestic responsibilities are prioritized. Consequently, academic demands are not met, lectures are missed, deadlines extended and, not infrequently, penalty systems come into operation and marks are lost.

Women academics often empathize with the plight of the students they work with because we do share aspects of their situation. Yet our status and salary cushion us against its sharper edges. In many ways this complex position of empathic identification and privilege creates in us a willingness to engage more fully with our pastoral role than the realities of mass higher education allow. For just as women's studies students find it difficult *not* to care for those in *their* communities, women academics experience internal and external pressure to provide care for those in *our* 'community' made up of the very diverse students who enrol on our courses. Many of us, for personal and political reasons, would not have it any other way. But in common with our women students we know that the care we provide is fragmented, unsupported and piecemeal.

It was probably always the case. We are both aware that the system of higher education has rarely approached either learning *or* the learner from a truly holistic perspective (Reeves, 1988). Such a perspective would include a willingness to recognize that the ability to benefit from higher education depends as much upon the student's personal circumstances as upon any intellectual qualities they might possess. The personal tutor system of the past was imperfect but there *was* usually someone there to listen to our academic and sometimes personal woes. As tutors we also believe that there was a time, not so long ago, when we knew all our students' names, the courses they were taking and whether, by and large, there were any major problems impinging on their academic progress. We operated, in short, in a system short on corporate rhetoric but relatively abundant in the practice of pastoral care. Such care mattered and it was a validated part of our role as tutors.

Yet 'pastoral care' with its allusions to vague ecclesiastical roots was always, in some ways, problematic. Whilst it sat easily with the ethos of 'liberal' and 'person-centred education', it always generated a dismissive sneer from those who valorized the product over the process. Although having its historical origins in a highly paternalistic model of clerical patronage, the modern practice of 'pastoral care' has been *maternal* rather than *paternal*. Jenny Shaw's work on the parental role of school teachers (in *'loco parentis'*) shows that in common with many families the empirical parent doing the parenting is the mother not the father (Shaw, 1995). Just like primary and secondary education, 'pastoral care' was very often 'maternal care' irrespective of the tutor's gender. Currently, the rhetoric of mass higher education valorizes 'the student experience' (but not over managerial control) whilst ensuring that any care that is provided is 'maternal care' carried out by feminized and often lower status staff. In our experience, the 'dismissive sneer' has escalated, often with support from the management, into a 'bullish', often full blown roar of disapproval.

As tutors we have been encouraged to reconsider the amount of time we devote to 'pastoral care' of students. We have increasingly been encouraged to accept that in the present 'educational climate' such care is a luxury 'we' cannot afford. The 'we' here is, of course, problematic and begs the question which 'we'? As tutors we have been exhorted to see that time we give over such care is time lost from administration and, more importantly, the manufacture of products, that is, research. It is no longer in our best interests to devote time to students. Indignant at such advice we have resisted. For one thing it is not easy to make one's living out of analysing women's oppression whilst refusing to listen to a woman student's account of her own oppression. But resistance isn't easy and it's getting harder. The projected cut backs for higher education, with their implications for early retirement and redundancies, suggest that it will get harder still. 'We ain't seen nothing yet!'.

Care has increasingly become a 'maternal', feminized feature both in the wider community and in the communities of higher education. Whilst there are many respected male colleagues who practise it alongside us, we know that this aspect of our and their work is feminized and devalued. In the anxiety-driven context of higher education involvement in 'women's work' is polluting and has the potential to contaminate others by association. Academics seeking promotion must adopt 'masculine work practices' (Coppock, Haydon and Richter, 1995, p. 87), fostering relationships and developing skills which are recognized, valued and bring maximum reward. Managerial tasks and research count more highly than pastoral care. Viewed as rational, unemotional enterprises, they are allied with a 'masculinized' model of task accomplishment and completion, the quality of which can be scrutinized, policed and quantified. Care remains, as it always has been, qualitative, process oriented, ongoing and unmeasurable. Highly subversive of masculinist models of work, caring engages with what has been called 'body time' rather than 'work time' (Martin, 1987). Devoting time to student welfare is increasingly regarded as 'time out' from proper time, that is, time for research, management, administration (Richards, 1996). Recognition that the academic progress of students is contingent on their social and economic well being is submerged in the name of parity. Those who do not meet assignment or examination dates must have documented 'evidence' and narrow definitions of 'extenuating circumstances' are acceptable to Examination Boards. Personal tutors find themselves colluding in the medicalization of social problems or urge an appointment with the student counselling services. They do so because academic judgment no longer counts. Circumstances must be documented, medical certificates obtained, letters from doctors and counsellors sought and kept on file. The irony of valorizing professional opinions from medical practitioners and counsellors over personal tutors does not escape us, nor the fact that managers give precedence to these when making academic decisions.

Thus, academic failure is explicable in terms of individual failure. Just as the poor are blamed for their poverty, the homeless for their homelessness, so those who fail educationally are blamed for their failure to maximize their opportunities in the post-modern lottery of higher education. This lack of a holistic vision concerning student, tutor and the learning experience is particularly at odds with those of us working within the ethos of women's studies education. For here our students' experience not only counts, it forms part of the basis of their education.

'I Know You're Busy, But . . .'

Tutors and students alike are exhorted by the corporate rhetoric to engage in time management. We are even offered courses to assist us in this endeavour to manage time more 'efficiently'. Time for research is to be jealously guarded against time devoted to student welfare issues such as crèche provision, woman-friendly time-tables or the replacement of class notes torched by an insecure male partner. (The cremation of lecture notes is *not* just restricted to 'Educating Rita'.) Students observe us scrimping, saving and hoarding our time. They recognize what we are doing. They too expend time saving time. They approach us, if they approach us at all, with tentative overtures such as 'I know you're very busy, but . . .', 'This won't take long . . .' etc. Their relative powerlessness in the fact of our structurally created greed for time is manifested in statements of gratitude for having 'had' some of 'our time'. It is evident that the less powerful are bound to honour the more important time of those further up the educational hierarchy. There is a mythology amongst some members of staff that students' time is not valuable (Adam, 1990). Yet it is clearly the case that their lives are even more complicated than were the lives of their counterparts a decade ago. Thanks to community care policies their family commitments are often greater than in the past. Student poverty means that they have to balance paid work (sometimes full-time, shift work) with full-time education. The very real impoverishment confronting students ensures that, for many of them, education is only a small but significant feature of their working day. It is not uncommon to be served in the supermarket at the end of our working day by the very same students who have just attended our lectures. For them the working day has just begun.

Thus, their time and our time is shot through with demands from inside and outside the university. Yet in order to benefit from higher education, students must be 'proper students' whose time is organized around lectures, seminars and private study. 'Proper students' are not expected to have other major commitments and, if they do, these must not interfere with the demands of education. If combining education, family and work results in problems which seriously affect their academic progress, their 'ability to benefit' is questioned. Thus, the 'ability to benefit' implicitly endorses individual responsibility and, it follows, individual blame.

Rosalind Edwards' (1993) study of mature women students suggests that their perspectives on their relationships with their lecturers were informed by accessibility and availability. Lecturers who had time for students were appreciated as people who cared about them. As women's studies lecturers, we agree that students should feel able to talk to us about personal problems if they wish and it seems ironic that at the very same time that 'pastoral care' is being relegated, student demand for care increases as the stresses in their lives become intolerable. We endeavour to be accessible and available and to know something of our students' lives outside the university. However, we find ourselves caught in the middle of a student need which sometimes feels infinite and institutional demands that we produce finite goods in the shape of academic papers, articles and books. In our own university a leaflet from Welfare Services advised personal tutors that, whilst it was not our place to counsel students, we should ensure that students did not feel abandoned if we referred them onto another agency. In the week we received this document, we also received a memo asking us to list our research accomplishments over the last few years. In the face of such contradictions it is not surprising that both tutors and students complain of confusion, fatigue and helplessness.

Disempowering Personal Tutors

In discussion with colleagues, we have found that many of us feel 'ineffective', 'inept', 'untrained', 'unskilled', and 'inappropriate' to deal with the diverse problems brought to us by students. It is not uncommon for tutors to express a sense of profound 'loneliness' in their role. Rules pertaining to confidentiality may increase this sense of loneliness. Whilst interpretations of what confidentiality actually means this may vary in practice from tutor to tutor, most colleagues subscribe to its value in some form or another. Like carers in the family there is often no-one to share the problem with either because confidentiality precludes it or because colleagues are otherwise engaged. Counsellors, paid and voluntary, have a network of supervision to assist them. No such network is available to personal tutors unless it has been created informally amongst themselves. Supporting students through periods of stress arising from, for example, bereavement, homesickness, depression, domestic violence, may have a profound impact on their ability to complete the course (a quantifiable product at last!). Yet this support is invisible and unsupported. Caring for a colleague's welfare whilst they are extending care to a student is 'time out', time taken away from real work. It does not appear on our time-tables. It does not appear on our self-appraisal forms. It is disappeared alongside our work with students. It is indicative here that pastoral care no longer appears on staff time-tables in many institutions.

For those tutors who resist, they are left feeling that they are not doing 'what really counts'. The tutor is seen as operating according to a feminized system of values whilst working in a masculinized framework. We would suggest that *whatever* the sex of the tutor they are perceived as acting as an 'academic cissy' and they had better shape up and act more 'like a man'. It is futile for us to complain to line managers about feeling deskilled around student distress as we shouldn't be getting involved in the first place. It seems that within a masculine ethos concern with process spells marginalization, concern with products ensures a place in a very visible centre (of excellence!). Having little talent for, and less interest in, student pastoral care is rarely an obstacle to promotion or a reason to withhold academic reward. This activity, which is rarely visible and cannot be measured, has no value and no return.

Conclusion

These problems are, we would suggest, encountered by any academic staff who still subscribe, however tenuously, to the liberal ideals of education or the more radical ones of theorists such as Freire (1972). As such we are the so-called dinosaurs of education. In the post-modern world we are allegedly as 'old hat' as socialism, feminism, trade unionism and welfare rights. In rolling back the 'Nanny State' there are those who would have us roll over each other in a bid not to be pushed to the bottom of the social pile. For us as feminist academics, the ironies are both ironic and cruel. In attempting to value and empower those who have traditionally occupied a subordinate position, we find ourselves driven by the corporate ethos of expediency and efficiency. In the prevailing moral climate 'investing in people' appears to be tantamount to invalidating the person, the personal and the political.

References

ADAM, B. (1990) *Time and Social Theory*, Cambridge: Polity Press.

BRANNEN, J. and MOSS, P. (1991) *Managing Mothers: Dual Earner Households after Maternity Leave*, London:Unwin Hyman.

COOPER, C. (1996) 'Hot under the Collar', *Times Higher Education Supplement*, 21 June, p. 15.

COPPOCK, V., HAYDON, D. and RICHTER, I. (1995) *The Illusions of 'Post-feminism': New Women, Old Myths*, London: Taylor and Francis.

COTTERILL, P. (1992) '"But for Freedom, You See, not to Be a Babyminder": Women's Attitudes towards grandmother Care', *Sociology*, **26**, pp. 603–18.

COWELL, R. (1996) 'The new model university for the millenium', *Times Higher Education Supplement*. 25 August, pp. 12–13.

EDWARDS, R. (1993) *Mature Women Students: Separating or Connecting Family and Education*, London: Taylor and Francis.

FINCH, J. and GROVES, D. (1983) *A Labour of Love: Women, Work and Caring*, London: Routledge and Kegan Paul.

FISHER, S. (1994) *Stress in Academic Life: The Mental Assembly Line*, Buckingham: Society for Research in Higher Education and the Open University Press.

FREIRE, P. (1972) *Pedagogy of the Oppressed*, London: Penguin.

GRIFFITHS, R. (1988) *Community Care: An Agenda for Action*, London: HMSO.

LEWIS, J. and MEREDITH, B. (1988) *Daughters Who Care: Daughters Caring for Mothers at Home*, London: Routledge.

MARTIN, E. (1987) *The Woman in the Body: A Cultural Analysis of Reproduction*, Milton Keynes: Open University Press.

MORRIS, J. (1993) *Independent Lives: Community Care and Disabled People*, London: Macmillan.

QURESHI, H. and WALKER, A. (1989) *The Caring Relationship: Elderly People and Their Families*, London: Macmillan.

REEVES, M. (1988) *The Crisis in Higher Education: Competence, Delight and the Common Good*, Buckingham: Society for Research in Higher Education and the Open University Press.

RICHARDS, H. (1996) 'Part-timers fill lecturing gap', *Times Higher Education Supplement.* 10 November, p. 7.

RITZER, G. (1993) *The McDonaldisation of Society*, Newbury Park: Pine Forge.

SAUNDERS, C. (1995) 'Poor students rush for advice', *Times Education Supplement* 22 September, p. 3.

SEEGER, P. (1992) 'Lady, what do you do all day?', in SEEGER, P. *Songs of Love and Politics*, Smithsonian/Folkways Recordings.

SHAW, J. (1995) *Education, Gender and Anxiety*, London: Taylor and Francis.

UNGERSON, C. (1987) *Policy is Personal: Sex, Gender and Informal Care*, London: Tavistock.

WALKER, A. (1993) 'Community care policy: From consensus to conflict', in BORNAT, J. et al. (eds) *Community Care: A Reader*, London: Macmillan in association with Open University Press, pp. 204–27.

2 From Earthquake Zone to Firm Ground: Challenging the Ideology of Heterosexism in Health and Social Work

LesleyAnne Ezelle and Lindsay Hill

Introduction

This paper is a discussion of our experiences as women and feminists working and teaching sexuality and sexual identity in the field of health and social work. Teaching in this area not only requires that students understand the very complex theoretical and practice issues at a personal and professional level, but that they are also able to transfer theories into practice to enable them to work more effectively at an individual and structural level. Vocational training is explicitly about the process of grounding theory in practice; about the relationship between theory and lived experience. Thus, teaching sexuality and sexual identity within this context requires the student not only to develop an understanding of how patriarchal heterosexuality is structurally manifest and how this impacts upon the individual, but to apply this knowledge to their work with service users. Achieving this is difficult, since from our experience, we would argue that there is an absence of a theoretical and practice discourse that acknowledges and celebrates lesbian and bisexual women's lifestyles and identities. Rather, if a discourse exists, it is concerned with promoting and maintaining a model of Traditional Familialism (Redman, 1994) which results in either ignoring or pathologizing alternative lifestyles and experiences. This paper aims to identify the struggles involved in introducing an epistemology of sexuality into the curriculum that brings together the theory and lived experience of different sexual identities and behaviour. This inevitably involves challenging patriarchal heterosexuality and exploring the implications for lesbian, bisexual and heterosexual women. We will start by discussing what we understand the context of teaching and learning to be in our substantive areas, with reference to the influence that current changes in higher education have on inclusion and celebration of diversity.

In our work with students, we have sought space and a framework that will enable us both as teachers and learners to analyse our specific and shared experiences and to acquire knowledge that will enable us to feel more confident and discerning in the choices that we make in both our personal and professional lives. We are also striving to find ways to explore the synergy between theory and experience in the quest to find a discourse that enables women to explore, and possibly find a way of coping with, the conflicts between the lived and constructed experience (Vance, 1989). This requires a structure or framework that acknowledges and accommodates the elements of, and tensions between, pleasure and politics (Vance, 1989). To help us understand our experiences we have developed a way of looking at our current teaching and learning situation and conceptualize this as the 'earthquake zone' (Figure 2.1). In attempting to secure a sense of integrity and honesty in our work we have developed strategies for change which we conceptualize as 'firm ground' (Figure 2.2). We discuss this model in greater detail later in the chapter. One of the risks associated with attempting to develop a discourse that takes into account the personal and the political, is that it can become prescriptive. We would want to resist this, and therefore offer our analysis and current ideas (acknowledging that these may change and alter with learning and experience) for trial and debate.

The Current Context of Teaching and Learning: What Has Sexuality Got to Do with It?

Broadly, vocational training, in the area of social and health care, seeks to provide the student with the necessary skills and knowledge that can be applied effectively in the practice setting. In the case of social work training, values and attitudes are a fundamental aspect of the curriculum, with the student required to demonstrate anti-discriminatory and anti-oppressive practice (Central Council for Education and Training in Social Work, 1991) which by definition, explicitly includes sexual orientation. Thus, there appears to be a mandate, particularly in the area of social work training, to provide students with the opportunity to examine their own values and attitudes, but also to develop skills and knowledge that would enable them to work from an anti-heterosexist perspective. This would be manifest as *acknowledging* diversity of sexual identity; *celebrating* the experiences, choices and lifestyles of lesbians, gay men and bisexual people and *empowering* through facilitating and supporting those seeking services. However, even with a directive to address anti-discrimination and anti-oppression, the social work curriculum is imbued with patriarchal heterosexism (Ezelle et al., 1996a; Brown, 1992). This results in *ignoring* the importance and significance of sexuality and sexual identity; *pathologizing* non-heterosexuality; and finally *prescribing* traditional heterosexuality as the acceptable and normal expression of sexual identity. We would suggest that the problem results firstly from structural heterosexism that is part of the framework of organizations and secondly with a lack of an objective 'body of knowledge' that is inclusive and accommodating of diversity. The emphasis and importance placed on the family further exacerbates the problem, since the 'family' is interpreted in the traditional sense (Beechey, 1985), with lesbians and bisexual women being considered unsuitable for parenting (Radford and Cobley, 1987; King and Pattison, 1992). It is commonly accepted that social work and nursing imports a 'body of knowledge' from other disciplines to equip students with the knowledge that can be applied to and make sense of complex human experiences. However, this 'body of knowledge' is historically derived from theories and research that has either excluded lesbian and bisexual women (Brown, 1992) or pathologizes the experiences and needs of non-heterosexual women (Kitzinger and Perkins, 1993; Kitzinger, 1990). Furthermore, women's sexuality is obscured, since their needs and experiences are described and accommodated in relation to men's sexuality. Anything that challenges or cannot be accommodated by the definition of men's sexuality is either rendered invisible or pathologized (Carabine, 1992). For black women there is an added dimension in that racism also becomes an issue as they seek to validate their choices in a culture that already views their sexuality as uncontrollable and therefore in need of regulation (Bryan et al., 1985). The impact of this ideology of patriarchal heterosexism, coupled with racism, means that students are unlikely to be provided with the chance to explore or examine sexuality and sexual identity outside of the model of traditional familialism.

Women Teaching Women: The Pleasures and Pains

Teaching sexuality not only brings the opportunity for engaging in and supporting others in developing self awareness and exploring possibilities for change, but also the difficult and often painful aspects of exposure and misrepresentation. We have found teaching sexuality can bring both pleasure and pain to us as teachers, but also to the student, as we collectively grapple with making sense of, and finding alternatives to, patriarchal heterosexuality. The courses and sessions we offer on sexuality tend to be very popular, with participants seeking to explore and further understand the link between theory and lived experiences as it is applied to their personal and professional lives.

From our experience, it is primarily women who attend courses in sexuality and sexual identity. This is partly due to the organizational structure of health and social work education and provision. There are more women than men who are attracted to the caring services, which is reflected in the classroom. Another important point is that it is more often women who remain in the role of carer, whereas men take on the role of manager (Grimwood and Popplestone, 1993). However, we would also suggest that it is not simply an organizational issue, but that men assume they are the holders of sexual knowledge and therefore do not need to explore issues further. Seidler (1987) suggests that since the Enlightenment male heterosexuality in western society has been identified with 'reason', whereas femininity is thought to embody 'irrationality' and 'unreason'. Sexuality as a taught and lived body of knowledge is equated to irrationality and unreason, therefore is not only academically suspect but also threatens the control that males strive to maintain in their personal and professional lives.

The commitment of organizations, both Education and Health/Social Services, to provide learning opportunities in sexuality is ambivalent. Hearn and Parkin (1987) in their discussion of sexuality in organizations point out that within the context of organizational life, sexuality is considered to be biologically and socially part of the private domain, specifically relegating sex to the family; whilst organizational life is part of the public domain. Sexuality and sexual identity courses straddle both the private and the public domains as students examine and critique their own experiences as well as issues related to social policy and social care provision. Models of health and social care centre around the ideology of the family, which reproduces traditional roles (Clements, Clare and Ezelle, 1995) and patterns of power and dominance (Craft and Brown, 1994). Thus the role of men is to define sexuality, but it is women's role, as carer, to understand and regulate the expression of sexuality within the boundaries of patriarchal heterosexuality. When the lecturer introduces a perspective of sexuality and sexual identity that is outside of the traditional family model, there is the likelihood of a clash between the objectives and expectations of the lecturer and the organization. Rather than supporting the public/private split and the ideology of traditional familialism, we seek to enter into a dialogue where both teacher and learner deconstruct patriarchal heterosexuality and push out the boundaries to facilitate a broader and more challenging view of personal and organizational sexuality.

The family model is integral to social work and health organizations with sexuality being expressed within the stable confines of married life; this results in childless women and lesbians being often ignored (Rosa, 1994). Furthermore, coupled heterosexual women, particularly if children are a result of the relationship, are expected to remain monogamous; though this expectation is not extended to coupled heterosexual men (Rosa, 1994; Sheppard et al., 1995). For women, non-monogamy or even intimate friendships are considered suspect and in some instances deemed unacceptable. As women students begin to deconstruct patriarchal heterosexuality and challenge oppression, they find a sense of accomplishment and empowerment as they begin to discover new ways of working. This often involves more collaborative practice. In one of our groups, two women were able to work together in order to bring about a change in policy which recognized and supported the rights of women with learning difficulties to explore their own sexual identity rather than have it defined for them. However, unless support is offered to women, either through networks or direct line management it is easy for them to lose momentum and become discouraged; the danger is that women can be isolated and marginalized within an organization that is ambivalent about its role and commitment to anti-heterosexism.

Carole Vance (1989) argues that both the pleasures and dangers of sexuality need to be personally and politically examined, though the tensions and paradoxes may never be resolved. For women the issue of 'pleasure' and 'danger' become more apparent, when a concept of 'choice' is introduced. Traditional models of heterosexuality often prescribe women's sexuality in relation to 'procreation' (Parrinder, 1987). The 'choice' issue, on the one hand, suggests the possibility of 'enjoyment' for women — on the other it can identify the point of divide, when particular 'choices', which are deemed less valuable, also become equated with something which is ethically and morally wrong, as is the case with lesbians, abortion, contraception and divorce. The tensions need to be made explicit in order that women can engage in an inquiry that pushes out the boundaries of sexuality. Since it is necessary to engage women as both 'subject' and 'object', facilitating and attending the workshops can be experienced as 'challenging' and/or 'dangerous'. There are often assumptions about members being 'feminist lesbians' — those who challenge male power. Heterosexual women in these situations can feel more precarious in relation to their sexual identity. When sexual identity is politicized in this way it challenges women's personal identity, which can be liberating for some, demoralizing and hurtful for others. We are aware that there is an absence of language around hetero-sexuality for women which is not related to lesbian or patriarchal identity (Kitzinger and Wilkinson, 1993) and we feel it is necessary to enable women to find space to address the conflicts that can occur within themselves and in their relationships with other women. We have personally experienced anger from women who felt that we were promoting a lesbian life style, rather than a women's right to choose. The anger is also associated with a growing awareness of the structural oppression experienced by heterosexual women. We have noticed in particular that where women are working with those who have been victims of abuse, the issue of male power, and the dangers inherent in this for women, create a feeling of vulnerability, from which women may prefer to be distanced.

We believe that educationalists should seek to create an informed, positive and valuing educational culture that enables students to reflect upon and learn from their similarities and differences. Women as participants in 'oppression' need to examine their contribution in a manner that does not regress into anger and hostility against other women. Morley (1993, p. 127) suggests that heterosexual women when con-fronted with their role as oppressor respond in anger as they 'engage with the subject from their hurt'. She goes on to say that in her experience 'women were concealing their hurt and vulnerability by revealing their anger and thus appearing to react from a dominant position' (Morley, 1993, p. 127). We would suggest that it is not simply 'hurt' but also a painful and frightening realization that there exists an irresolvable conflict between the personal and political, which results in feelings of helplessness and vulnerability. Whilst the 'hurt' is directed at other women learners, the situation, to some extent, can be contained. However, when learners locate the responsibility for the conflict with the teacher, anger and hostility may spill outside of the classroom and can be perilous for both the teacher and lesbian students. Though women as 'oppressors' find it discomforting to be confronted with inequality, Morley (1993, p. 127) found that 'the differences exposed in the exploration of the larger social/ political issue allowed a clear focus on power and process within the group, and the relationship between macro- and micro-systems of prejudice, misinformation and domination'. Women, both as oppressor and oppressed, can learn from this and pos-sibly begin to find a personal resolution between the lived and constructed experience.

Developing a Discourse for Teaching and Learning

The argument being developed so far is that teaching on sexuality and sexual identity, particularly where teachers and students are women, often takes place in the context informed by patriarchal heterosexuality, where the aim is to uphold and maintain the traditional face of the family. This perspective creates a tight and restricted view of sexuality, with alternatives either being ignored or silently acknowledged in disdain. The impact of this upon workers who try to introduce another discourse, is that they may find themselves in an 'earthquake zone' (see Figure 2.1). We conceptualize this as a place where the prevailing ideologies,

Figure 2.1: Earthquake Zone

Few practical skills
Limited knowledge
Workers/teachers discriminated against
Lack of concern about valuing differences

structures and practices are oppressive to the kind of change which is required to value and support differences in lifestyles. Thus the earthquake zone is dangerous for both teachers and learners, since external and internal events can sabotage or destroy the learning opportunities. We would suggest that the earthquake zone is characterized by the following individual and structural variables that contribute to maintaining patriarchal heterosexisms:

- a lack of knowledge concerning the value of diversity;
- limited skills of working outside of the patriarchal framework;
- absence of an effective equal opportunities policy;
- climate of mistrust between staff and students;
- no shared understanding of what sexuality and sexual identity is.

We found the model helpful for the following reasons:

- It helped to alert desensitized students to issues of power and discrimination that exist at both a personal and political level.
- It enabled those students who were aware of discrimination to place their experiences within a conceptual framework which acknowledged the personal and political complexities of their lives.

In our workshop on sexuality and sexual identity we have experienced women struggling to make sense of their own conflicting experience of women as sexual beings. As previously stated, this has been of particular relevance in situations where women as social workers and health workers have been involved in working with women and children in areas of domestic violence and sexual abuse. Part of the problem is that practitioners are not provided with the discourse and framework, through their training, that would enable them to make sense of and find an alternative perspective to patriarchal heterosexism. The importance of having a language around sexuality which women own for themselves, and which is not imposed by patriarchy is vital if both workers and clients are to be empowered to make decisions about their own lives. However, in the current climate of 'moral panic' which sees traditional family life and therefore, traditional morals under threat, it can seem very threatening to adopt a language that challenges patriarchy. Anger and frustration can spill out as students recognize that in order to support client choice they will be required to challenge what is 'natural' and 'normal', as defined by a patriarchal society. This can make them vulnerable on a personal and professional level.

The earthquake zone has been responded to as a familiar place when women talk about their experiences of violence, victimization and confusion. The exploration of economic, political and cultural factors as they affect the nature of the relationship between sex, gender and sexuality within the 'earthquake zone' challenges the individual pathology model, which has sought to make women responsible for containing male sexuality and male violence. By identifying and exploring the features of the 'earthquake zone' as it is experienced by women, we aim to create movement from a position in which women blame themselves or each other for not being 'good enough' to one where the complexity of sexuality and its intrinsic links with power relations in society begin to be identified. Students are encouraged to explore relationships and social policy, asking questions about why, for example, single women or lesbians are often deemed as unfit mothers.

We were concerned not to limit our aims solely to the identification of the 'earthquake zone' as we felt this would continue to be disempowering. Teaching and learning should operate as a vehicle for change not merely as an insight-giving exercise, limited by concerns to maintain the status quo. Earthquake zones, as the terminology suggests, are never static. Recognizing that sexual order is always changing (Weeks, 1985) provides the optimism through which strategies for change can be identified. We conceptualized the change in terms of 'firm ground' (Figure 2.2), the position that we, along with our students, would seek to move to during the

Figure 2.2: Firm Ground

Knowledge based on research/experience
Competency in skills: teaching/learning
Commitment to competency in anti-discriminatory practice
Trust/confidence in professional relationships
An open acknowledgment of the dynamics of power

experience of being involved in the programme. The 'firm ground' model is located in a value system which is designed to promote equality and social justice. It involves a way of working which incorporates a specific commitment to change both on a personal and political level. The components of 'firm ground' were identified as being:

- knowledge;
- skills;
- trust and confidence;
- set within a framework of an effective equal opportunities policy;
- an open acknowledgment of the dynamics of power.

In terms of knowledge, we would suggest that there is a baseline of knowledge which people need to have that moves along the spectrum from the personal to the political. This knowledge base which proposes that sexuality and sexual identity are 'politically' and 'socially' constructed, is essential to enable the recognition and critique of the dominant discourse of heterosexuality. This is a particularly important area for women since, as previously stated, heterosexuality as lived and constructed experience, has been largely defined by heterosexual males, with the control of patriarchy. Women's bodies, as Adrienne Rich (1979) suggests, have been heavily controlled and regulated by male power, which is manifest through the institution of compulsory motherhood and compulsory heterosexuality. In social work where the majority of clients are women, we have examples of how white middle class male power, when vested in the state, denies women access to resources such as childcare facilities and family planning, and yet holds women responsible when children are deemed to be at risk (O'Hagan, 1995). A knowledge base which not only recognizes the complexities of sexuality and sexual identity, but also places this within the context of unequal power relations between women and men, is essential to the development of anti-oppressive practices.

It is also essential that in developing a knowledge base, we do not substitute one interpretative frame for another. As Vance (1989) has suggested there is no universality about sexual meaning. We are not, as previously stated, searching for another form of prescriptionism. It is vital to recognize that students bring with them their own cultural frame, connections and personal experience. The workshops need to provide the context in which knowledge can be created, when political, social, economic, historical and personal perspectives begin to intersect with one another. It is through debates about women's sexuality that we can move towards a way of thinking about sexuality which can be empowering for women. Sexuality comes to be understood as a multiplicity of experience which acknowledges difference; a difference in which women have rights in terms of defining their own sexuality and thus being able to make choices, rather than being constantly objectified as victims.

In enabling students to make sense of the knowledge, as it applies to themselves both personally and politically, we are also aiming to develop the *skills* which are essential for working in this area. Principally we aim to encourage reflective practice, in which planning, action and evaluation are essential ingredients (Schon, 1989). The emphasis on action, moves the experience from one which is a theoretical exercise, to one which requires knowledge to be transferred into practice. We are becoming increasingly aware that students require skills which promote social action as a vehicle for change. Group work and advocacy skills, skills in presentation, argument and analysis are all essential for students to feel sufficiently confident to take these issues back into what is often, a 'hostile' workplace.

The third area which has been identified as being a component of 'firm ground' is trust and confidence. As facilitators we seek to create trust and confidence in our students. Experiential work which values difference and encourages discussion is essential. We offer students a workbook, on which they can start to focus before they begin the programme. This provides them with opportunities to explore their own awareness of their language and attitudes towards sexuality, before they arrive. In this sense we are making it explicit from the beginning that understanding sexuality is as much about understanding and valuing the 'lived experience' as it is about exploring theoretical models. This pattern of personal exploration and the analysis of material is evident throughout the programme.

The 'firm ground' model thus helped us to identify not only what students required, but also what we as females were required to facilitate the development of practice skills in the area of sexuality and sexual identity. In terms of its application to a model for teaching we were able to identify three strands which could be translated into objectives for teaching and learning, namely that students should be able to:

- reflect on and critique the theoretical discourses around sexuality and sexual identity;
- examine the personal and political interface;
- construct and evaluate a project that addresses issues of sexuality and sexual identity in the workplace.

An evaluation of the teaching and learning based on personal reflection and student feedback helped us to identify a number of essential issues that we consider important to address in order to enable students to move onto 'firm ground'. These issues are especially relevant where students are on professional/vocational training programmes and are thus required to make explicit links between theory and practice.

Framework of Support to Enable Student to Move to 'Firm Ground'

Students need support and advice that will enable them to address the power dynamics that operate at a personal and organizational level. It needs to be recognized that women in a patriarchal culture are frequently sexualized as 'objects'. Therefore taking issues back into the workplace draws attention to the student and makes her sexuality more public and open to speculation and discussion. When lesbians attempt any work with lesbians, motives can be 'judged' as being self-oriented and therefore suspect. The role of the teacher is extended as she attempts to find strategies to support the development of learning through practice. We felt that the following strategies could be useful in enabling students to feel more competent and confident.

- Contracts with managers: A prerequisite to attending the programme is that students gain written support from their line managers. This includes not only a commitment to releasing them for study but also for creating and supporting opportunities for learning to be taken back into the workplace.
- Team teaching: Opportunities need to be created to enable a shared value and knowledge based in teams who are collectively working towards implementing anti-oppressive practice in the area of sexuality and sexual identity.

We would like to see opportunities for teachers to move into the practice settings to facilitate a whole team approach towards teaching and learning.

- Buddy system: Support between students both during and after the programme was found to be invaluable in enabling people to sustain commitment towards challenge and implementation of the learning. Students can be encouraged to identify with like-minded people with whom they can continue to maintain links after the completion of the programme.
- Joint project work: Students found it invaluable to work with another person on their project, since it enabled them to have a broader perspective and gain support, particularly in situations where the work environment manifested features of the 'earthquake zone'.

Individual students need different levels of input, therefore it is important not to make assumptions concerning the levels of skills, knowledge and self awareness. For some, the workbook and group activities exposed personal and professional difficulties which needed to be examined in a safe and non-confrontational environment. Again we stress the importance of gendered groups being available to students in order that they can explore the impact of material. Students who are heterosexual need to be supported in building a political analysis which enables them to support their own choices.

In terms of the personal/political interface, students need to have the opportunity to explore the various options available to them within their role and the implications for them personally and professionally. The material may trigger unresolved issues for individuals; support services need to be available.

Conclusion

In this paper we have attempted to present our struggles to teach sexuality and sexual identity in the field of health and social work and to suggest a model for teaching and learning. We have been arguing for the development of a way of teaching and learning about sexuality and sexual identity which challenges the discourses in relation to female sexuality which promote female victimization and favour married heterosexual states over other sexual choices. Our theoretical approach has been to attempt to:

- understand;
- deconstruct traditional understandings about sexuality and sexual identity;
- create a framework which enables us to move towards a position where we can begin to celebrate difference;
- identify the support structures which both teachers and students require in order to be able to work more creatively in this area.

Working in this area takes its toll. The stigmatization which can occur as a consequence of challenging heterosexist practice has to be recognized. The dialogue which is being developed with students also needs to be matched by dialogue between faculty members. It is vitally important that equal opportunities policies actively support teaching and learning in this area. One final lesson, we cannot demand of our students is that they do more than we are prepared to do ourselves.

References

BEECHEY, V. (1985) 'Familial ideology,' in BEECHEY, V. and DONALD, J. (eds) *Subjectivity and Social Relations*, Milton Keynes: Open University Press.

BROWN, H. (1992) *Working with the Unthinkable: Abuse of adults with learning disabilities*, London: Family Planning Association.

BRYAN, B., DADZIE, S. and SCAFE, S. (1985) *The Heart of the Race*, London: Virago.

CARABINE, J. (1992) 'Constructing women: Women's sexuality and social policy,' *Critical Social Policy*, **34**, pp. 113–26.

CENTRAL COUNCIL FOR EDUCATION AND TRAINING IN SOCIAL WORK (CCETSW) (1991) *Rules and Requirements for the Diploma in Social Work*, Diploma-Social Work, Paper 30.

CLEMENTS, J., CLARE, I. and EZELLE, L. (1995) 'Real men, real women, real lives?: Gender issues in learning disabilities and challenging behaviour,' *Disability and Society*, **10**, 4, pp. 425–35.

CORIN, C. (1994) 'Fighting back or biting back?: Lesbians in higher education,' in DAVIS, S., LUBELSKA, C. and QUINN, J. (eds) *Changing the Subject: Women in Higher Education*, London: Taylor and Francis.

CRAFT, A. and BROWN, H. (1994) 'Personal relationships and sexuality: The staff role,' in CRAFT, A. (ed.) *Practice Issues in Sexuality and Learning Disabilities*, London: Routledge.

EZELLE, L. and HILL, L. (1996a) 'Developing a discourse for teaching sexuality,' Conference workshop, *Sexual Politics in Higher Education*: University of Northumbria.

EZELLE, L. and HILL, L. (1996b) 'Women teaching sexuality: Developing a discourse for teaching sexuality,' Conference workshop, *Women in Higher Education Annual Conference*, University of Central Lancashire.

GRIMWOOD, C. and POPPLESTONE, R. (1993) *Women, Management and Care: Practical Social Work Series*, England: Macmillan.

HEARN, J. and PARKIN, W. (1987) *'Sex at Work': The Power and Paradox of Organisation Sexuality*, England: Wheatsheaf Books.

KING, M.B. and PATTISON, W. (1987) 'Homosexuality and parenthood,' *British Medical Journal*, **303**, 3 August, pp. 295–7.

KITZINGER, C. (1987) *The social construction of lesbianism*, London: Sage.

KITZINGER, C. and PERKINS, P. (1993) *Changing Our Minds: Lesbian Feminism and Psychology*, England: Only Women.

KITZINGER, C. and WILKINSON, S. (1993) 'The precariousness of heterosexual feminist identities', in KENNEDY, M., LUBELSKA, C. and WALSH, V. (eds) *Making Connections: Women's Studies, Women's Movements and Women's Lives*, London: Taylor and Francis.

MORLEY, L. (1993) 'Women's studies as empowering of "non-traditional" learners in community and youth work training: A case study,' in KENNEDY, M., LUBELSKA, C. and WALSH, V. (eds) *Making Connections: Women's Studies; Women's Movements and Women's Lives*, London: Taylor and Francis.

O'HAGAN, K. (1995) *The Abuse of Women within Child Care Work*, Milton Keynes: Open University Press.

PARRINDER, G. (1987) 'A theological approach,' in GEER, J. and O'DONOHUE, W.T. (eds) *Theories of Human Sexuality*, New York: Plenum Press.

PLUMMER, K. (1992) 'Speaking its name: Inventing a lesbian and gay studies,' in PLUMMER, K. (ed.) *Modern Homosexualities of Lesbian and Gay Experience*, London: Routledge.

RADFORD, J. and COBLEY, J. (1987) 'Lesbian custody project on social work reports rights of women,' *Bulletin*, May.

REDMAN, P. (1994) 'Shifting ground: Rethinking sexuality education,' in EPSTEIN, D. (ed.) *Challenging Lesbian and Gay Inequalities in Education*, London: Open University Press.

RICH, A. (1979) *On Lies, Secrets and Silence*, New York: Virago.

ROSA, B. (1994) 'Anti-monogamy: A radical challenge to compulsory heterosexuality,' in GRIFFIN, G., HESTER, M., RAI, S. and ROSENEIL, S. (eds) *Stirring It: Challenges for Feminism*, London: Taylor and Francis.

SCHON, D. (1989) *The Reflective Practitioner*, London: Jossey Bass.

SEIDLER, V.J. (1991) *Recreating Sexual Politics: Men, Feminism and Politics*, London: Routledge.

SHEPPARD, V.J., NELSON, E.S. and ANDREOLI-MATHIE, V. (1995) 'Dating relationships and infidelity: Attitudes and behaviours,' *Journal of Sexual and Marital Therapy*, **21**, 3, pp. 202–12.

VANCE, C. (1989) 'Pleasure and danger: Toward a politics of sexuality,' in VANCE, C. (ed.) *Pleasure and Danger: Exploring Female Sexuality*, USA: Pandora.

WEEKS, J. (1985) *Sexuality and Its Discontents: Meanings, Myths and Modern Sexualities*, London: Routledge.

WINTER, R. (1989) *Learning from Experience*, London: Falmer Press.

3 Surviving the Institution: Working as a Visually Disabled Lecturer in Higher Education

Sally French

Introduction

This chapter documents my experiences as a visually disabled lecturer over a period of 20 years.[1] These experiences are grounded within a broader discussion of the employment situation of disabled people, particularly visually disabled people in Britain today, exploring factors which prevent our full inclusion in paid employment. This discussion will highlight the social model of disability, promoted by disabled people themselves, where disability is viewed as a civil rights issue rather than a medical issue.

Visually Disabled People and Employment

Disabled people are far more likely to be unemployed than non-disabled people and the situation is particularly bleak for black disabled people and disabled women. Oliver states:

> Labour markets in the developed world continue to discriminate to the point where disabled people are three times more likely to be unemployed that their able-bodied counterparts . . . On any indicators disabled women and black disabled people fare worse than their white male counterparts. (1996a, p. 115)

Many disabled people regard paid employment as a major aspect of their struggle for equality (Abberley, 1996). As well as the many benefits employment can bring — social status, friendships, a sense of purpose, the opportunity for self development — it also provides an income which may help to counter some of the many disabling barriers disabled people face.

The employment rates of visually disabled people are particularly low. In 1991 the Royal National Institute for the Blind (RNIB) published the first nationwide survey of visually disabled adults in Britain (Bruce et al., 1991) where it was found that only 25 per cent of visually disabled people of working age were in full or part-time employment compared with 31 per cent of disabled people. Bruce et al. point out that 'not being in paid employment is normal for visually impaired people of working age' (1991, p. 235).

Table 3.1: *Occupational status*

	Professional	**Semi-skilled and unskilled**
Visually disabled people	14%	36%
Disabled people	25%	31%
Non-disabled people	34%	23%

Source: Bruce, McKennel and Walker, 1991

In a more recent study Winyard (1996) found that the unemployment rate among visually disabled people was two and a half times the national average. He cites a survey by the Institute of Employment Studies where over half of employers said that they would not employ someone who had 'difficulty in seeing'. Winyard concludes that 'visually impaired people are seen as the most difficult group to employ amongst British disabled people' (1996, p. 22). This is confirmed by the RNIB (1996) who state that: 'visually impaired people suffer from employment discrimination more than any other disablement group'.

Despite the reluctance to employ disabled people, there is some evidence to suggest that they are more efficient and competent than other employees, that they stay longer in a job, take less sick leave, and are more conscientious (The Local Government Management Board, 1991). Similarly, The Royal Association for Disability and Rehabilitation (RADAR) (1993) found that disabled workers were equal or better than non-disabled workers on productivity, attitude to work, and attendance.

The good work record of disabled people may reflect a severe lack of employment opportunities, as well as feelings of insecurity and vulnerability. Disabled people may feel a need to 'compensate' for disability and to 'prove themselves' because of adverse stereotyping or the fear of losing their jobs. As a blind woman quoted by Shearer states:

> I feel I have to be really good, not ill often and always producing my best. I don't want to give anyone the chance to criticise me or think I cannot cope because of being blind, it can be quite exhausting. (1981, p. 45)

Visually disabled people are far less likely to be in professional jobs than non-disabled people or other disabled people (Bruce et al., 1991; Winyard, 1996). This is illustrated in Table 3.1 which draws on two separate surveys. There are approximately 3,000 visually disabled people in professional jobs in Britain today, of whom a small minority are lecturers in higher education. It is not possible to state their precise numbers, for as Hurst states, 'disabled staff (in higher education) are an "invisible" group in any work that has been done so far' (1996, p. 128).

To help make sense of the discrimination disabled people experience at work, and to show the way forward to our inclusion, it is helpful to discuss briefly two central models of disability.

Models of Disability

The individual model of disability is based upon the assumption that the problems and difficulties disabled people experience are a direct result of their individual impairments (Swain et al., 1993). This view has been promoted by the health and welfare professions and is often referred to as the medical model. Disability is viewed in terms of disease process, abnormality, and personal tragedy with the assumption that both the problems disabled people experience and the solutions to them lie within disabled people themselves rather than within society. This view is seen to operate in the medically based assessments which are used for recruitment in most types of employment. Ryan and Thomas state:

> Medical model thinking tends to support the status quo. The subnormality of the individual rather than the subnormality of the environment, tends to be blamed for any inadequacies. (1987, p. 27)

The individual model of disability is prevalent in higher education where disabled students and particularly disabled employees are expected, largely, to find solutions to what are regarded as *their* problems. If assistance is offered it is usually on an individual basis, as something 'special', rather than any real attempt being made to alter the practices and structures of universities to accommodate disabled people. Attempting to modify the workplace for individual disabled people, if and when they appear, rather than making the environment accessible on a planned basis, is not useful; at best these modifications take a long time to occur, at worst they do not happen at all. In my present job it took a year before an office with suitable lighting was found and after two years I still do not have computer equipment which I can use — it is interesting that a visually disabled male colleague has not had to wait so long.

There is ample evidence that disabled people's views on disability thoroughly contradict those of non-disabled people (Swain et al., 1993; Campbell and Oliver, 1996). Oliver (1990) believes that whereas disability is viewed by non-disabled people as stemming from the functional limitations of impaired individuals, disabled people believe that they stem from the failure of the social and physical environment to take account of their needs and rights. He regards disabled people's views as constituting a social model of disability, where the problems are seen, not within the individual disabled person, but within society. Thus the visually disabled person is not disabled by lack of sight, but by lack of braille, cluttered pavements, and stereotypical ideas about blindness. Finkelstein (1981) has argued that non-disabled people would be equally disabled if the environment was not designed with them in mind.

With the growing influence of the Disabled People's Movement and the persistent demand for civil rights from disabled people over the past 20 years, the social model of disability has gradually become more influential and led in 1995 to the passing of the first *Disability Discrimination Act* in Britain which became law in December 1996. Although the legislation is weak, with many exemptions and no sound enforcement mechanism, Gooding (1995) describes its introduction as 'a fundamental shift'. Winyard states:

> The Act places important new requirements on employers and has the potential to open up new opportunities for blind and partially sighted people and people with other disabilities. Whether it does make a difference to the long standing and deep seated discrimination they have faced in the labour market depends primarily on the response of employers. (1996, p. 24)

It also depends on how far the legislation is enforced. The enforcement of the quota scheme introduced in the 1944 Employment Act was ineffective, resulting in few prosecutions and low fines. The new legislation, however, demands albeit in a limited way, the removal of barriers to employment for disabled people.

Barriers to Employment

The social model of disability explains the problems disabled people experience as resulting from three types of barriers which interact — environmental, structural and attitudinal. Environmental barriers refer to physical obstacles, such as cluttered corridors, uncovered holes, and lack of essential facilities such as braille, large print and adjustable lighting. Structural barriers refer to the way organizations are run, for example the way meetings are conducted and the time allocated to travel or to undertake specific tasks. Attitudinal barriers refer to the adverse attitudes and behaviour of others towards disabled people. Disabled people experience these barriers in many aspects of their lives, including employment. Talking of visual impairment Bradfield states:

> While much emphasis has been placed on the acquisition of basic skills required to perform tasks, it has become increasingly obvious that the impact of external or environmental factors plays an important role in the ability of the worker to perform the job. In fact, these factors, if not attended to, may prohibit otherwise qualified workers from obtaining employment. (1992, p. 39)

Attitudinal barriers often lie at the root of environmental and structural barriers and the absence of disabled people within the workplace, or witnessing the struggles disabled people face in a disabling environment, may serve to strengthen and justify these attitudes — if disabled people are not present or appear to struggle it may be assumed that they cannot do the job. On the other hand, if disabled people are seen to be coping this has the potential to change attitudes in a positive direction although it may lead to simplistic notions that the disabled person is 'just like everyone else'. Attitudinal barriers are frequently covert and are, therefore, difficult to identify and challenge. Employers may ask for capabilities which disabled people have not had the opportunity to acquire, or ones which are not really needed, such as the ability to drive a car. These are all examples of indirect discrimination.

As a visually disabled lecturer in higher education I encounter numerous barriers on a daily basis. These barriers have been present wherever I have worked and have not reduced over the years; in fact, in many ways, as the institutions have become larger and more impersonal, they have worsened, despite the rhetoric of 'equal opportunities'. These barriers are numerous and include inaccessible computers, lack of large print, unsuitable lighting, inaccessible inservice training, punishing time schedules, inaccessible information on notice boards and lack of adaptation at meetings. Farish et al. (1995) point out that Equal Opportunity Committee meetings are, in themselves, frequently inaccessible. This has been my experience where, as well as being unable to see the material displayed on the overhead projector or read at the necessary speed the numerous documents being passed around, I sometimes do not even know who is present. None of this is to imply that individual people are deliberately unhelpful — in fact I rarely experience overt attitudinal barriers — but that universities as institutions do nothing to welcome or assist visually disabled lecturers.

Barriers to the employment of visually disabled people exist outside the workplace too. Lack of a good public transport system may lessen the choice of where we can work, and the necessity to cross a busy road, without a pedestrian crossing or an underpass, can present a serious obstacle. Hanging around at bus stops after evening teaching sessions can put us in risky situations which our colleagues who drive do not have to face.

The discrimination I and most disabled people experience within higher education is institutionalized, that is it is embedded within the very fabric of university life. This makes it difficult to challenge and difficult for well-meaning people to help or to alter their behaviour.

Coping with Barriers

One development that has occurred over the past 15 years is the provision of services, paid for by government, to assist disabled people at work. Equipment such as specially adapted computers are now available as well as money to pay for personal readers. Roulstone (1993) points out that technology has the potential to widen the range of employment possibilities, as well as the tasks disabled people can do. Technology may also alter perceptions of disabled people, from those of dependency to those of efficiency and independence. This in turn has the potential to shift the meaning of disability from the individual to the environment. These services are, however, currently under threat and are increasingly being eroded (Westminster Round-up, 1996).

As a lecturer I have used magnification software with a large computer monitor for 10 years in various institutions and it enables me to carry out tasks which otherwise I could not do unaided. It does not, however, remove disability or solve the problems of working in a disabling environment. My working speed is still very slow and there is no help from the computer department if anything goes wrong with the 'special' equipment. I have no access to on-site computer training, nor money to pay for my own, and the magnification does not work well with software such as E-mail. As technology becomes more and more 'part of the job' in higher education, disabled lecturers, rather than being enabled, may be increasingly disabled.

Access to technology for disabled people is not generally uppermost in the minds of employers, which means that when technology is introduced there is no guarantee that it will be used in an enabling way. Oliver (1990) contends that little attention has been given to the potential of technology to *remove* barriers to employment. It may appear that the provision of 'special' equipment is a move towards organizing work to take into account the needs of disabled people, but initiatives such as this are generally geared towards 'normalizing' disabled people and making us productive and acceptable to employers regardless of our own particular needs as employees (Oliver, 1990). The provision of technology is usually the preferred option over reorganization of work.

Equipment can also disable people because once it is installed we may be expected to cope without any human assistance which can be difficult. Since technology for visually disabled people has been installed in university libraries, for example, I have found that librarians are less inclined to help even though coping on our own is slow, inefficient and frequently partial (French, 1994).

Technology and human help with reading has, then, been the major response of government to assisting visually disabled people at work. The RNIB also has a reading service where material is read on to tape free of charge. These services, individualistic though they are, have been useful to me, but my major strategies for coping as a visually disabled academic have been to work longer hours and to avoid promotion with its inevitable increase in administrative work. As I have never been in a position to negotiate my role I have avoided administration by remaining in relatively junior positions.

Human help from colleagues is also important but very haphazard. Sometimes a helpful and perceptive secretary or technician can make an enormous difference but visually disabled people should not be obliged to rely on the goodwill of others. We need to feel confident that working in a barrier-free environment is our right and that we will receive the same treatment and facilities wherever we work so we are not afraid to progress through the organization or to change jobs. I have found that although academics give and receive help from each other all the time, it is not generally acceptable for visually disabled colleagues to ask for help with tasks such as marking or reading. The provision of technology, for example talking computers, has exacerbated this problem by tending to remove whatever human help previously existed.

Even health and safety legislation does not take into account our needs as disabled people. Recently I was approached at work by a 'health and safety officer' who was checking the seating and posture of all the staff to ensure we were 'ergonomically sound' when working with computers. None of the advice he gave applied to me (I do not have a computer at work) yet when I asked if he could do anything about the hazardous outdoor environment he suggested that I contact the 'works department'. With regard to health and safety legislation, disabled employees are only ever regarded as a threat in terms, for example, of evacuation in the case of a fire.

Barnes (1996) mentions three coping strategies he has used as a visually disabled academic — minimization (minimizing disability), over-compensation (trying to perform at a higher level than other people) and openness. I too have used all three strategies but, in the climate of life in higher education institutions at the present time, I find openness the most problematic and dangerous strategy to use. It places demands on employers which they may not welcome and can lead to adverse labelling of disabled people. Baron et al. (1996) refer to the reluctance of disabled people to disclose their impairments and disabilities as 'manoeuvres in self-defence' which, though entirely rational, can serve to maintain or increase the barriers. Some attempt has been made to address the discrimination disabled people experience at work, however, by the use of equal opportunities policies.

Equal Opportunities

'Equal opportunities' is not an easy term either to define or to translate into practice, with the result that equal opportunities policies tend to concentrate on relatively straightforward matters, such as interview practice, recruitment, and monitoring the numbers of disabled employees in the organization. Little attempt has been made to organize work so that disabled people can participate in it on an equal level with their peers in higher education (Farish et al., 1995). The restructuring of work, for example to give visually disabled people more time to perform it, or to eliminate the need to drive, is rarely considered (French, 1994).

The issue of time is important for visually disabled academics as, whatever equipment we use, our reading and working speeds are slower than those of non-disabled colleagues. It is also considerably slower to read braille or to listen to tape than it is for sighted people to read print. In addition, as Dodds points out, reading 'involves the person in a lot of effort. Great amounts of concentration are required to extract useful information and this is tiring.' (1992, p. 34) This makes tight deadlines particularly stressful and has, on several occasions, prevented me from becoming an external examiner, because institutions are not flexible enough to give me a little more time to read the students' scripts or to use the services of a reader. I am not, therefore, able to play a full role in academic life. Baron et al. (1996) point out that most disabled people, regardless of impairment, need more time to carry out tasks.

Farish et al. (1995) conducted case studies of colleges and universities in Britain, highlighting how equal opportunities policies for disabled people were not as highly emphasized as those for women or people from ethnic minorities and, where they did exist, were mainly directed at students. Financial constraint was frequently cited as a problem and a large gap between rhetoric and practice was evident. They state:

> Disability is another area that has received relatively little attention particularly in relation to staff . . . there was little pressure to promote the perspectives of staff

with disabilities and there has been no history of awareness training in the issue. (1995, p. 72)

I always feel sceptical when lack of resources is used as a reason for not removing disabling barriers — how much would it cost to paint a few white lines on steps? So often it is a case of priorities, with the needs of disabled people being low on the list. In one university where I worked I was denied sufficient finances to support disabled students adequately or to meet my own needs and yet I was sent to distant cities on course promotion exercises where little expense was spared.

Equal Opportunities statements, good interview practice and quotas can very often lull disabled people into a false sense of security, rendering us less able to make an informed choice. This happened to me in a university which has a good reputation on the inclusion of disabled students. I discovered when in the post, however, that the organization would not accommodate me. I found myself trying to read microscopic print and appalling handwriting or going to meetings where none of the information was in an accessible format for me. I could not see the numbers or names on the doors and found the layout of the campus confusing, a problem which was exacerbated by inaccessible signs. I found myself yearning for the 'bad old days' when, though dialogue was blunt ('you can work here provided you manage like everyone else'), we, as visually disabled individuals, knew exactly where we were!

This lack of activity in relation to disabled employees is not helped by government literature which perpetuates the notion that disabled people are 'just like everyone else' and therefore do not need any help or support. The document *Ability Counts*, states, for example, that:

> Most disabled people will not have any special needs and any necessary equipment and assistance can easily be obtained . . . in most ways they will be no different to any other workers you employ. (The Local Government Management Board, 1991, p. 3)

It is, of course, convenient for employers to believe that we want to be treated 'just like everyone else', yet as Oliver states, '. . . the disability movement throughout the world is rejecting approaches based upon the restoration of normality and insisting upon approaches based upon the celebration of difference' (1996b, p. 44). Disabled people are demanding the right to be as they are.

The idea that the attitude of employers is the most significant barrier to the employment of disabled people is also commonly expressed. On various occasions over the years I have been asked to take part in disability awareness sessions for university staff. These events are invariably poorly attended, mainly by the converted few, and never result in any tangible change. I am always left convinced that the money would have been better spent painting white lines on steps or putting clear labels on doors. This is not to imply that the dissemination of knowledge about visual disability and attempting to change people's attitudes is unimportant. It is my experience that little is known about visual disability, particularly its diversity, and that we tend to be stereotyped. I have, on occasions, been compared with other visually disabled staff, though our situations and the barriers we face are very different.

Continually campaigning and arguing for our rights as lone disabled people with little or no support from others is time-consuming and exhausting. The fear of being labelled 'difficult', with all the implications for working relationships, references and promotion in the very competitive academic world, leads many disabled people, myself included, to remain passive much of the time.

Equal opportunities policies are overwhelmingly about gender and race with disability being 'tagged on' almost as an afterthought (Baron et al., 1996). These policies have done little but raise expectations with minimal result and often exist primarily to present a positive and progressive image of the organization, to provide 'a smoke screen behind which the status quo remains largely unaffected' (Farish et al., 1995. p. 180).

Conclusion

When I was asked to write this chapter I hesitated because I knew it would be rather negative and this made me feel uncomfortable. As disabled people we are socialized not to complain. Focusing on problems can also be depressing, especially when little is achieved. It is difficult to write critically about our employers and colleagues as we are particularly vulnerable to accusations of 'having a chip on our shoulder' and thus having our experiences disqualified. We are also a very small minority and therefore lack the safety of numbers. We do not want to alienate managers and colleagues and, by doing so, make life more difficult for ourselves. Yet the pressure to accept our situation, to make light of it and not to complain is a substantial part of the problem. Only last week I heard a colleague say, 'I really like those two dyslexic students, they don't make a big thing of it, they just get on with it and don't winge.' We too are expected to minimize the difficulties we face and compensate for them. We are not encouraged to draw attention to disabling barriers; indeed, to do so can have very serious consequences (French, 1993a).

Visual impairment gives rise to substantial barriers which cannot readily be changed by environmental or social manipulation. These include our inability to recognize people and to respond to non-verbal communication (French, 1993b). However, most of the barriers we experience as lecturers in higher education could be reduced or resolved if the political will to do so existed. Nothing inherent in visual impairment prevents us from being 'good academics'; I love to write and research, I do not experience difficulties when teaching and I know that my experience and academic interest in disability, though marginalized, is highly relevant in the area of health studies where I work. Academic life has had a major and positive impact on my self-identity, personal growth, self-esteem and my satisfaction in life; I have always felt that being a lecturer in higher education is the right occupation for me, but as a visually disabled woman academic I pursue it at considerable cost to myself.

Note

1   I would like to thank Maureen Gillman and John Swain of the Faculty of Health, Social Work and Education, University of Northumbria, who read and commented on an earlier draft of this chapter.

References

ABBERLEY, P. (1996) 'Work, utopia and impairment', in BARTON, L. (ed.) *Disability and Society: Emerging Issues and Insights,* London: Longman.

BARNES, C. (1996) 'Visual impairment and disability', in HALES, G. (ed.) *Beyond Disability: Towards an Enabling Environment,* London: Sage.

BARON, S., PHILLIPS, R. and STALKER, K. (1996) 'Barriers to training for disabled social work students', *Disability and Society,* **11**, 3, pp. 361–77.

BRADFIELD, A.L. (1992) 'Environmental assessment and job site modification for people who are visually impaired', *Journal of Vocational Rehabilitation,* **2**, 1, pp. 39–45.

BRUCE, I., McKENNELL, A. and WALKER, E. (1991) *Blind and Partially Sighted Adults in Britain,* The RNIB Survey, London: HMSO Publications.

CAMPBELL, J. and OLIVER, M. (1996) *Disability Politics: Understanding Our Past, Changing Our Future,* London: Routledge.

DODDS, A.G. (1992) *Rehabilitating Blind and Visually Impaired People,* London: Chapman and Hall.

FARISH, M., McPAKE, J., POWNEY, J. and WEINER, G. (1995) *Equal Opportunities in Colleges and Universities: Towards Better Practices,* Buckingham: The Society for Research into Higher Education and Open University Press.

FINKELSTEIN, V. (1981) 'To deny or not to deny disability', in BRECHIN, A., LIDDIARD, P. and SWAIN, J. *Handicap in a Social World,* Sevenoaks: Hodder and Stoughton.

FRENCH, S. (1993a) 'Can you see the rainbow?: The Roots of Denial', in SWAIN, J., FINKELSTEIN, V., FRENCH, S. and OLIVER, M. (eds) *Disabling Barriers — Enabling Environments,* London: Sage.

FRENCH, S. (1993b) 'Disability, impairment, or something in between?', in SWAIN, J., FINKELSTEIN, V., FRENCH, S. and OLIVER, M. (eds) *Disabling Barriers – Enabling Environments,* London: Sage.

FRENCH, S. (1994) 'Equal opportunities? — Yes please', in KEITH, L. (ed.) *Musn't Grumble: An Anthology of Writing by Disabled Women,* London: The Women's Press.

GOODING, C. (1995) 'Employment and disabled people: Equal rights or positive action', in ZARB, G. (ed.) *Removing Disabling Barriers,* London: Policy Studies Institute.

HURST, A. (1996) 'Reflecting on researching disability and higher education', in BARTON, L. (ed.) *Disability and Society: Emerging Issues and Insights,* London: Longman.

THE LOCAL GOVERNMENT MANAGEMENT BOARD (1991) *Ability Counts,* London.

OLIVER, M. (1990) *The Politics of Disablement,* London: Macmillan.

OLIVER, M. (1996a) *Understanding Disability: From Theory to Practice,* London: Macmillan.

OLIVER, M. (1996b) 'Defining impairment and disability: Issues at stake', in BARNES, C. and MERCER, G. (eds) *Exploring the Divide: Illness and Disability,* London: Policy Studies Institute.

ROYAL NATIONAL INSTITUTE FOR THE BLIND (RNIB) (1996) 'Out of sight — Out of work?' *The New Beacon,* **80**, 947, pp. 23–4.

ROULSTONE, A. (1993) 'Access to new technology in the employment of disabled people', in SWAIN, J., FINKELSTEIN, V., OLIVER, M. and FRENCH, S. (eds) (1993) *Disabling Barriers — Enabling Environments*, London: Sage.

RYAN, J. and THOMAS, F. (1987) *The Politics of Mental Handicap*, London: Free Association Books.

SHEARER, A. (1981) *Disability: Whose Handicap?*, Oxford: Basil Blackwell.

SWAIN, J., FINKELSTEIN, V., FRENCH, S. and OLIVER, M. (1993) (eds) *Disabling Barriers — Enabling Environments*, London: Sage.

THE ROYAL ASSOCIATION FOR DISABILITY AND REHABILITATION (1993) *Disability and Discrimination in Employment*, London: The Royal Association for Disability and Rehabilitation.

WESTMINSTER ROUND-UP (1996) *New Beacon*, **80**, 948, p. 23.

WINYARD, S. (1996) *Blind in Britain: The Employment Challenge*, London: Royal National Institute for the Blind.

4 Women, Social Work and Academia

Lena Dominelli

Introduction

Social work, traditionally defined as a women's profession associated with voluntary work and the 'labour of love' (Graham, 1983), reflects the transposition of patriarchal relations from the private sphere to the public domain. It has a low professional status (Flexner, 1915; Heraud, 1979) and continues to struggle for its rightful place in the academy. Its dependency on the state for the funding of its practice has made it vulnerable to political exigencies and government dictat. The combination of a financially dependent status and association with 'women's work' has endangered the serious evaluation of the activities undertaken by staff in social work education, training and practice (Dominelli, forthcoming).

The low regard for the knowledge base, skills and expertise of social workers has provided the context which has shaped developments in social work and contributed to the undervaluing of the activities social work educators undertake. It has also fuelled the view that social work does not quite fit into the academic framework. The failure of social work to establish itself as a high status discipline has led to a self-fulfilling prophesy in which the expectations of social work are limited and become limiting.

In this paper, I examine the tenuous hold social work has in academia by looking at the position of its members of staff from the standpoint of both the discipline and women, and making links between the two. I conclude by positing that strengthening the position of social work practitioners and academics needs to go hand in hand with enhancing the position of service users. Moreover, for social work academics to effectively defend their right to remain in academia, they need to secure a broad coalition of support within the academy. This will require them to create alliances with sympathetic cognate disciplines and others offering professional qualifications. In the short-term, this will also mean social work will have to perform well according to the same criteria being used to judge other disciplines. As these are 'man-made' because men dominate in the upper echelons of the academy, men's agendas will once again determine the parameters within which social work will be evaluated and may mean that the discipline, given its different structure and lower status may lose out. In the longer term, by remaining within the academy, women social work educators can influence the definition of academic excellence and ensure that existing views about professionalism are revised in ways that recognize and support women's aspirations in creating high quality alternatives.

The Academy, Women and Social Work

The predominance of women at the lower levels of social services departments and amongst the ranks of service users is well-known (Howe, 1986; Hallett, 1989; SSI, 1991). The Central Council for Education and Training in Social Work (CCETSW) collects figures showing the number of men and women students on qualifying courses. These demonstrate that women traditionally substantially outnumber men. Although there was a period in the mid-1970s when the proportion of men students on social work qualifying courses rose dramatically, men's interest in applying for these has been declining in recent years. Today, there is a disparity in the ratio of women students to men of 3 to 1. Moreover, social work courses require students to be over 21 years old. This means many of them are mature students with family commitments. For women students, this often means juggling child rearing and elder care alongside their studies and makes survival on student grants and loans a difficult proposition.

The pattern of limited male involvement in social care is being replicated in the NVQ training. Here, men are even more conspicuous by their absence. Less has been written about the position of women social work educators in the academy. There has been no comprehensive national examination of this issue. The global employment figures collected by the Department of Employment and the relevant trade unions do not provide a breakdown specifically for social work, let alone, gender and other social divisions such as 'race'. Consequently, there is little empirical evidence to draw on. The invisibility of social work and its neglect as both a discipline and a profession is glaringly obvious.

However, there have been a few studies which can shed light on this matter. Research carried out under the auspices of the International Association of Schools of Social Work (IASSW) has revealed some interesting patterns which indicate that the bulk of social work academics at lecturer level in western industrialized countries other than Israel, are women, while those at (full) professorial level are men. In Israel and the industrializing countries of the Third World, most social work academics are women, but so are the (full) professors (Dominelli, 1986). This suggests that academic posts offering greater professional status and higher salary levels are more easily accessed by and attractive to men. Moreover, men successfully capture the bulk of jobs in the top echelons of the labour hierarchy in disproportionate numbers. This pattern has also been confirmed by studies undertaken during the early 1990s in Canada by the Canadian Association of Social Work and the United States by the Council of Social Work Education. This trend is also one which Howe (1986) found prevailed in the field in Britain where men collared the higher status and better paid managerial posts. Men, it seems are considered natural heirs to the business of managing people and resources.

Moreover, the predominance of men at the top of the university ladder in social work reflects the position of men academics generally. Women professors in the 'old' universities in Britain form about 2 per cent of the professoriat whilst constituting 14 per cent of lecturers (AUT, 1992). Whilst social work is more representative at the top than other disciplines because it has more women professors, this disproportionality remains. More worryingly, women's position at the time of writing seems to be deteriorating. A number of chairs in social work are being lost to women. The abolition of the binary divide in British higher education in 1992 has strengthened men's position in this regard. A scrutiny of the membership list of the Association of University Professors in Social Work (AUPSW) reveals that before the polytechnics joined the universities, 15 per cent of its professoriat were women. Surprisingly, given the better record of the former polytechnics in employing women academics, the proportion of women professors declined to 12 per cent when AUPSW was enlarged through the admission of the relevant professors from the 'new' universities (AUPSW, 1994). The appointment of men without social work qualifications to manage large schools which encompassed social work divisions within a single cost and resource centre in the 'new' universities accounts for a large part of this reduction.

Women's position is fluid because a number of chairs remain to be filled, but this change mimics that which occurred in the field following the Seebohm reorganization of social services (see Seebohm, 1968). It also resulted in large bureaucracies in which men managers replaced women (Walton, 1975). The loss of women from the top echelons of academic life is likely to accelerate as the emphasis on research which is currently driving university agendas intensifies its impact on social work. Also, the recent casualization of academic labour has impacted more strongly on women who are the prime holders of part-time and sessional contracts without job security and few employment rights.

Despite these obstacles, social work has an enviable record of high achievers amongst its women professors. For example, Phylida Parsloe, Head of Social Work at Bristol University became the first woman pro-vice-chancellor in the 'old' university sector. Janet Finch, Head of the Social Work Course at Lancaster University, went on to Keele to become the first woman vice-chancellor at an 'old' university. Black men and women, however, remain under-represented in the university system at all levels.

Sadly, social work as a discipline has fared badly in the last two research selectivity exercises. As a discipline, social work will have to improve its rating above its previous poor average if it is to hold its own amongst other disciplines and secure its future research funding base and place in the academy. Fortunately, social work has done well in the recent teaching quality assessment exercise where 16 of the 70 courses visited in England and Wales were rated 'excellent'. The outcome of a similar exercise in Scotland is awaited.

A major reason for social work's poor showing in the research rankings are that traditionally, social work educators have put little emphasis on undertaking research which was not directly relevant to practice. This has meant that the opportunities to develop and foster a research culture in social work education have been limited. Additionally, social work educators' links with the field have resulted in inordinate amounts of academic time going into maintaining and developing these. But forging high quality contacts with services has been crucial for social work staff who count on the goodwill that they have developed with agencies to provide practice placements for students despite the financial straits most of them are in.

Besides these efforts, the supervision of students' professional development ties up considerable amounts of academic staff time. On a conservative estimate which does not allow for placements which are located beyond a 25 mile radius from the home base, I have calculated that placement support on a course seeing 80 students through one placement each per year requires 1280 hours of staff time annually. This amount of time is equivalent to one full-time member of staff. The fact that such a load is usually borne by a small staff group of usually five or six full-time equivalent members means that one-fifth of their academic time is unavailable for research purposes. This constitutes a research burden that is not carried by colleagues who do not have a professional qualification to teach alongside an academic one. Women are more adversely affected by these forces since they carry a dispropor-tionate share of the teaching burden. Moreover, many 'research active' men aca-demics are employing part-time women to undertake the professional support and supervision of their students alongside their teaching responsibilities to free up their 'more valuable' research time. Moreover, many sources of research funding specifically exclude social work. The British Academy and Leverhulme awards are well-known examples of this. The Economic and Social Sciences Research Council (ESRC) does not list social work as one of its discipline categories for the award of research studentships. Social work academics are poorly represented on the ESRC's decision-making structures and have been largely unsuccessful in bidding for research monies.

Much of the research that social work academics do is devalued regardless of their gender, although women are affected in larger numbers because there are more of them. Focusing on practical issues or those of an applied nature involving categories of people who carry little political clout and who are often despised by society at large, social work research is often discounted as 'proper' research, e.g., small-scale evaluation of a one-off project for women. Or, it may be of a sensitive nature and remains invisible because it comments on agency practices and is denied publication. Additionally, in the fine gradations which academics use to discriminate between different kinds of publications and publishers, those that appeal to a wide professional grouping are defined as 'unacademic'. Only reputable refereed aca-demic journals count as worthy of note on the positive side of the academic balance sheet. These ratings are also important to social work academics seeking promo-tion. Their research output can be downgraded if it has been published in an unprestigious journal or is intended largely for practitioner consumption.

Moreover, public expenditure cuts have reduced the funding which public sector employers and voluntary agencies can devote to research. A small sum of money nowadays is expected to go a long way. In stretching resources, skills that women have developed in the context of extending limited household resources to cover the needs of the whole family, are transferred to the research arena. These skills, however, can only cover a small portion of the gap, for the research will get done, but it is not accorded the recognition given to six-figure plus projects. The research agenda is also becoming more determined by the priorities of funders than it is by those of the independent researcher. These work against women whose interests focus on areas which have traditionally been neglected by those holding the purse strings.

Funding criteria usually favour the expenditure of significant sums of money on projects which rely on large-scale empirical research rather than more detailed small-scale ethnographic and qualitative methodologies, which are more appropriate for many of the subjects social work academics and practitioners investigate. These priorities exclude many 'cameo' portraits penned by feminist and black social work educators who prefer them because they allow a richer exploration of life experience and attitudes to service delivery (see Stanley and Wise, 1983). Thus, many of the practice insights emanating from feminist scholarship and black perspectives have come about via small-scale qualitative studies in which researchers are able to relate in more egalitarian ways to those who are the subjects of the research and provide the space wherein they can express their own voice (Reinharz, 1992). Often done with little or no 'independent' funding, these types of projects will be invisible in the quantitative money counting exercises indulged in by research selectivity exercises. This accounting method further marginalizes women's academic activities, a problem social work educators share with others, for example, women's studies.

Despite the disadvantages shackling social work academics, they are judged by the same yardsticks as their non-social work colleagues when the quality of their research and teaching is being assessed. To hold their heads up amongst colleagues, it is important that social work academics provide the same standards of excellence as their colleagues. But the realization of excellence does need to take on board the specifics of a discipline. This has not normally been done for research. However, the teaching quality assessment exercise did so to the extent that each course could define what 'excellence' meant to it and be measured against that standard. Since these definitions picked up on the specificities of social work teaching, the discipline did well vis-à-vis others. For a similar outcome to be effected in research rating exercises, it is vital that the gap in the starting line between social work academics and others is made visible. Without getting bogged down in special pleading, social work academics need to identify the unlevel playing field within which social work is located and ask that this be rectified — a call unlikely to be received favourably in a cost-cutting climate. Yet, despite the discipline's poor overall showing and notwithstanding the handicaps listed above, some social work departments have made the grade within the research accounting system used pre-1996. Two social work departments were rated '5' (the top mark) in both of the last two research selectivity exercises and a number '4'.

The 'Streetwise Granny' Approach to Social Work

The association of social work with the caring work which women do naturally has led to the view that anyone can do social work without needing to be adequately qualified or trained. Virginia Bottomley, as Secretary of State for Health, expressed this sentiment graphically when she said, 'any streetwise granny can do social work'. By suggesting that no training other than the acquisition of skills through the business of leading a 'normal' life and reaching a mature age is required to do social work, this belief devalues the complex work social workers do and sets the scene for trivializing their training needs. When acted upon at the highest political levels, it plays into strategies aimed at removing social work training from the academy as has happened in the case of probation (Sone, 1995). Lowering the status of social work teaching and removing it from its university base can conveniently assist the process of cutting educational expenditure. Moreover, developments in social work begin to provide the template for undermining the training needs of other caring professions currently located in academia, for example, speech therapy.

Withdrawing social work training from the university sector carries several other advantages for employers and government. Combined with the competency based approach to social work promulgated through the Diploma in Social Work (DipSW), it:

- lowers the costs of training individuals;
- denies academics control over the socialization of professionals;
- produces more compliant practitioners who are unlikely to challenge managerial prerogatives; and
- leads to the further fragmentation and deprofessionalization of social work.

This scenario is already evident in the developments emanating from community care, where a social work qualification is not a requisite for appointment at either care manager or practitioner levels. Indeed, employers have made it clear that they prefer social care assistants to hold a level 2 or 3 NVQ rather than a social work qualification, a position made possible by the absence of a regulatory body in the profession. In contrast, its regulated sister profession, nursing, is being welcomed into academia at the same time that social work is being pushed out.

The inservice training or NVQ route has the advantage of reducing the size of the employers' overall social work staff budget because NVQ qualified workers are doing tasks previously undertaken by professionally qualified people for less money. It also reduces employers' direct training costs because a worker can obtain an NVQ more cheaply in-house than going away for a professional qualification on an expensive college course for two years. Educational considerations about independence of thought, having time to step back and reflect on practice or being able to integrate theory with practice are largely irrelevant in this context.

Employers argue that NVQs give recognition previously denied to the training needs of a particular group of women and the work they do. In their view, this is a positive move which reflects their commitment to equal opportunities. A number of women agree with them on this point. However, I am concerned that NVQ training strategies lock women into an even lower paid ghetto than social work qualifications have hitherto done. In addition, by not being directly tied into or contiguous with academic awards, NVQs do not allow women to proceed automatically onto higher qualifications. This, too, devalues the training needs of women and their aspirations for high quality education and training. Also, by fragmenting complex professional tasks into competences, and making their acquisition (often via a check list) the be-all and end-all of training, NVQs lower further the status of the profession and intensify the deprofessionalizing processes social work education is already embedded within (Dominelli, 1996).

The downgrading of professional training and the deprofessionalization process is currently well-advanced in probation. Although the battle over it is ongoing, the Home Office has ceased to sponsor probation students on university courses and demanded that training be conducted in-house. The rationale the Home Secretary gave for this development was that probation was becoming too 'soft' and 'social workery' and needed to align itself with 'tough' professionals in the armed forces, police and prison services. In other words, the punishment of offenders was to supercede concerns about their welfare or prospects for rehabilitation, an aim more in keeping with the government's desire to turn probation into a corrections service (Sone, 1995). Moreover, the Home Secretary was concerned that there were too many women, single parents and black people becoming probation officers. Was he fearful that their 'natural' propensity to care for people who have been damaged by the material and emotional circumstances which shape their lives, would undermine his punitive and dehumanizing approach to offenders?

Ensuring that probation committees become responsible for training their own employees in-house will give employers control over the socialization process of these professionals. It will also lower the status and value of whatever qualification is secured in consequence. In-house awards are unlikely to be recognized nationally or internationally. But they will produce workers who can do the 'job' as stipulated by employers. 'Students' undergoing such training are unlikely to rock the boat if doing so might jeopardize their livelihood. The focus of their training will also become more narrowly vocational. As a result, competent technicians will replace capable reflective professionals who draw on a wide range of knowledge, skills and experiences to make difficult judgments about complex cases. On 'graduation', the technician will be more of a clone amenable to managerial dictat than the autonomous professional. Gendered language is being used to redefine the training agenda and shift the discourse away from caring about individuals to containing them. Through it, a more instrumental dialogue replaces an earlier expressive one. Ultimately, I expect a realignment of the probation workforce so that a lower ranking NVQ qualified probation service officer (PSO) undertakes jobs currently done by DipSW qualified probation officer (PO). Most POs are likely to be men; the PSO ranks will be comprised primarily of black and white women and black men. The shift to inservice training will reduce university demand for probation lecturers, trainers and practice teachers. These redundant educators are becoming self-employed consultants and NVQ assessors. Many of these redeployed positions are being filled by women who are now learning to survive on greater job insecurity and casualization — conditions that presage the feminization of probation education and training.

Notwithstanding these attacks on the profession, social work academics have been remarkably silent in defending their professional interests and failed to posit alternative paradigms for the public to debate. This silence can be partly attributed to the lack of a viable professional organization and the widespread belief that the profession should be accessible to as wide a group of people wishing to practice it as possible. The imperative for those arguing accessibility has been to resist attempts which might render the educational process elitist and closed to marginalized groups, especially working class white women and black people. These arguments have been significant in legitimating the proliferation of NVQs for people seeking qualifications in social care.

In their ideological zeal for it, employers and CCETSW have failed to recognize that the development of NVQ based training carries a number of dangers for social work by providing training for people who can be employed to do social work tasks on the cheap. These workers can save employers money in personnel costs because they are paid less than professionally qualified social workers. By doing the same work for less pay, these workers help to lower the status of the profession. Their lower status will also impact on their relations with higher status professionals when working on multi-disciplinary teams, and affect the weight their views will carry when they disagree. Besides contributing to the fragmentation of social work tasks and the deprofessionalization of practice, NVQs are contradictory in simultaneously providing women previously denied participation in training initiatives, access to training and educational support.

Surviving Academia As a Woman Social Work Academic

Women academics have a hard time in academia regardless of their discipline. However, the low status of social work exacerbates the problems that its women academics experience. The status of women's work, whether in teaching or research, will be called into question in a way that men's is not. This makes their experience of academia different from men's. Women professors will usually find themselves outnumbered in meetings by men professors, most of whom will have defined the educational agenda in very different terms from theirs. Many issues which women believe are important, men do not. Women's greater concern with process and feelings are indicative of these differences. As resourcing becomes more scarce, these tensions will become more strained and contentious than they were during affluent periods. The downgrading of teaching as an activity vis-à-vis research, the requirement to spend less time providing pastoral care for students, a halt in the development of more collaborative working relations in the workplace and the demand that secretarial staff take on more responsibilities without a commensurate increase in pay, are symptomatic of the gendered politics which are being enacted in academia at women's expense.

Men academics with a research orientation tend to be much more instrumental in their approach to the job and less preoccupied with what happens to each individual student or member of staff. They often assume that women colleagues will be primarily involved in teaching and ready to do the 'mothering' of the group, e.g., serve the tea, write the minutes of meetings, organize sessions, provide students with pastoral care, counsel staff through stressful times. Low paid women clerical staff are expected to nurture both staff and students. Women academic staff are asked to run courses with limited resourcing and administrative back up. Social work courses seem starved of cash in a way that the natural sciences are not. Indeed, there is often a direct subsidy through higher student numbers from the income generating 'soft' social sciences to the 'hard' sciences.

Also, the salaries of women academics at all levels are usually lower than those of men with comparable experiences and qualifications (AUT, 1992). This also constitutes a subsidy going from women to men whose higher pay exists because women's is lower. The remuneration problems of academic staff who have been in universities for a number of years without being considered for promotion are particularly acute. If they have reached the top of the lecturers' scale, they will drop behind in the pay scales as the years go by. In social work, the majority of these are women. Promotion constitutes one way of escaping the poor pay levels lower down the career ladder. Discussions with colleagues have revealed that women academics however, have a harder chance of getting recognition for their work and getting promotion. They have found that they are required to have more publications and research grants under their belts and been in post longer than their male colleagues before their cases are considered 'ready'. Despite their personal inclinations, many women have had to leave their institutions to seek promotion elsewhere. Men are more likely to be promoted where they are.

Moreover, the promotion criteria are highly geared towards research and publication. This makes advancement more difficult for women who prioritize teaching as is the case for a considerable number of those in social work. For women, then, the picture is one of constant struggle. Women academics are finding it harder to get their concerns and agendas accepted as legitimate ones for the academy to take seriously and address. However, doing nothing about women's complaints is unlikely to remain an option for university managers. Women are forming support groups and networks in which they can name their pain and use these to secure the changes they deem necessary. Because women lead very busy lives with the demands of work and home spilling into each other, the existence of these organizations is often fragmented and sporadic. But they are indicative of the ways in which women seek to develop more holistic approaches. The lack of funding to purchase support services augments the difficulties women encounter. Thus, as the example of the network for women social work academics set up at the Ruskin conference in the mid-1980s demonstrates, the attempts of women social work educators to network with each other have been less secure than many of us would wish. Nonetheless, collective action in support of each other is important in enabling women to move through the status of victims of patriarchal forces in which they adapt to the status quo to survivors in which they respond in their own defence to thrivers in which they are pro-active in promoting their own visions of the world. Moreover, women staff working in mixed settings like the university one, need to enlist the support of sympathetic men to improve the working environment not only for themselves, but for men staff and all students too. For although universities are gendered institutions, the current public expenditure cuts have a deleterious impact on all members of the university community regardless of gender (Dominelli and Hoogvelt, 1996). Moreover, in social work, some male academics endorse feminist aims and methodologies, thereby facilitating working together around specific objectives (see Bowl, 1985).

Conclusion

Social work's status in the academy suffers from being a discipline with a preponderance of women staff and students and concerned primarily with 'women's work'. Reversing the long-standing under-valuing of social work and the questioning of its place in the academy requires social work educators to find common cause with others. Women social work academics have a prominent role to play in advancing this project because they form the majority of the teaching staff and have a more holistic vision of education which universities need to take more seriously. However, given the low numbers of women in academia generally, women social work educators will need to also develop alliances with men across all sectors of the academy. Fortunately, many men are disgruntled with current trends in higher education. As the unit of resource continues to diminish and the pressures to produce more with less augment, men will also seek organizational change through collective action. This will facilitate the creation of alliances between men and women academics which can transcend discipline boundaries.

The attack on higher education is a struggle over who will control the curriculum: funders, including employers, or professional academics. Discussions about the future of the academy and the importance of intellectual independence in freeing creativity and getting the best out of people need to include their contributions too. Resolving conflicts initiated by the differing interests of employers and employees will call for creative dialogue to reach compromises which will be acceptable to all concerned. Women social work educators have networking expertise, knowledge and skills to take a lead in initiating such discussions.

Finally, many of the problems in higher education today are a direct result of the public expenditure cuts. These have dire consequences for students too. Academic staff should also be forming alliances with them. White women, black women and black men amongst the student group have lower access to financial resources both before and after training. Hence, they will suffer most under the impact of measures geared to making individuals personally pay for their education. As users, students can assist in the process of determining what happens in the institutions that they will call 'home' for several years. Their voice can be included amongst the chorus seeking to redefine universities as more egalitarian workplaces. In social work, the majority of students are women, many of whom are mature people with family responsibilities and commitments. They cannot neatly divide their lives into the private sphere of the home and the public domain of educational work. The two spheres are blurred in their reality and raise questions about crucial assumptions guiding university life, a key one being that students are single people aged between 18 and 21 with no worries other than their educational aspirations and who can survive at poverty levels. The presence of these students highlights the inadequacy of a grant system that presupposes low standards of living amongst students and a capacity to absorb large loans during their period of study and after graduation.

In short, women staff and students in social work help to expose universities as gendered hierarchical institutions. They will need to draw on the energies of all the constituent members of the academy to introduce changes which will give women staff and students a fair deal. Men will also benefit, if universities become better workplaces for women staff and students. For in these renewed institutions, men's needs as people whose lives span both the private and public arena can also be met. In other words, men's lives will be enriched as a result of attending to women's needs and supporting the agendas women place before them. The academy can be turned into a better place for all those working within it by improving the status of women in it. Social work academics and students, particularly their women members, have an important part to play in reaching this goal.[1]

Note

1   Lena Dominelli would like to thank those women who shared their ideas and thoughts with her.

References

ASSOCIATION OF UNIVERSITY PROFESSORS OF SOCIAL WORK (1994) AUPSW List, Dundee: University of Dundee, Department of Social Work.

ASSOCIATION OF UNIVERSITY TEACHERS (AUT) (1992) *Women Professors*, London: AUT.

BOWL, R. (1985) *Changing the Nature of Masculinity: A Task for Social Work*, Norwich: University of East Anglia Monographs.

DOMINELLI, L. (1986) *Women in Social Work*, Vienna: IASSW.

DOMINELLI, L. (1996) 'Deprofessionalising social work: Competences, equal opportunities and postmodernism', *British Journal of Social Work*, April.

DOMINELLI, L. (forthcoming) *Sociology for Social Work*, London: Macmillan.

DOMINELLI, L. and HOOGVELT, A. (1996) 'Globalisation, the privatisation of the Welfare State and the changing role of professional academics in Britain', *Critical Perspectives in Accounting*, **7**, pp. 122–91.

FLEXNER, A. (1915) 'Is social work a profession?', *Studies in Social Work*, **4**, New York: School of Philanthropy.

GRAHAM, H. (1983) 'Caring: A Labour of Love', in FINCH, J. and GROVES, D. (eds) *The Labour of Love: Women, Work and Caring*, London: Routledge and Kegan Paul.

HALLET, C. (1989) *Women in Social Services Departments,* London: Sage.

HERAUD, J. (1979) *Sociology in the Professions*, London: Open Books.

HOWE, D. (1986) 'The segregation of women and their work in the personal social services', in *Critical Social Policy*, **15**, pp. 21–36.

REINHARZ, S. (1992) *Feminist Methods in Social Research*, Oxford: Oxford University Press.

SEEBOHM, LORD (1968) *Report of the Committee on Local Authority and Allied Personal Social Services*, Cmnd 3703, London: HMSO.

Social Services Inspectorate (1991) *Women in Social Services*, London: SSI.

Sone, K. (1995) 'Getting tough', *Community Care*, 16–22 March, pp. 16–18.

Stanley, L. and Wise, S. (1983) *Breaking out: Feminist Consciousness and Feminist Research*, London: Routledge and Kegan Paul.

Walton, R. (1975) *Women in Social Work*, London: Routledge and Kegan Paul.

Section 2

Maternalism in the Academy

5   Mixing Motherhood and Academia — A Lethal Cocktail

Carol Munn-Giddings

> My children cause me the most exquisite suffering of which I have any experience. It is the suffering of ambivalence: the murderous alternation between bitter resentment and raw-edged nerves, and blissful gratification and tenderness. . . . I love them. But it's in the enormity and inevitability, of this love that the suffering lies.
> Adrienne Rich (77)

Introduction

Motherhood is central to my life and to many women's lives and identities. The feminist debate has revealed that motherhood is likely to be a crucial but sensitive part of women's lives, involving deep ambivalence in a central part of our self identities (Ribbens, 1994). Adrienne Rich's quote at the beginning of this paper, sums up, the richness, ambivalence and centrality of the experience of motherhood for me. Being a mother is integral now to my identity and my life and is both a source of oppression and liberation. It is both burden and joy and a continual responsibility — not something to be done before and after work or at weekends. It is not always a reciprocal relationship. It is however, a uniquely pleasurable relationship, through which I continue to learn and develop (e.g. vulnerabilities, strengths and weaknesses, interpersonal skills, self-reflection, negotiation, mediation). Thus while motherhood may at times be analysed as the cornerstone of women's oppression, recent feminist writers have been concerned to point out the ways in which it may also offer women the scope for an experience of active agency (Ribbens, 1994).

The demands of parenting, which vary at different stages of a child's development, and with different children, may potentially affect parents' ability and willingness to contribute in the workplace. Whilst many parents find it acceptable, if a struggle, to work full-time, overtime and evening commitments (whether this is a stated or cultural expectation) can prove to be both undesirable and unfeasible. Undesirable, because many parents want and have a responsibility to spend time with their children and unfeasible due to the difficulty and cost of arranging childcare. This can have particular implications for women, particularly for those in heterosexual relationships where for many there is still an unequal responsibility placed on women to be the primary carer for children. Moreover, whatever the childcare arrangements at home, it is still rare to find a working institution that does not implicitly and explicitly embody sexist assumptions that mirror the wider inequalities in society. As well as individual arrangements for childcare responsibilities within relationships, there is the necessity that both the state and individual organizations need to develop responsive mechanisms to enable parents to work on equal terms with their peers.

At first sight, this may not seem a particularly contentious or problematic statement to make. Many state initiatives and organizations, in response to feminist campaigns and to their own economic need have recognized this and developed appropriate mechanisms to enable parents to continue their valued input e.g. maternity and paternity leave, term-time contracts, flexible working hours, workplace nurseries, holiday playschemes, working from home (SSI, 1991). Although anecdotal evidence suggests that it is women who primarily utilize these schemes and that they are primarily located in middle-class professions, they appear effective in retaining women workers and offering them support in returning to and continuing work. The review of literature below, however, suggests that women with caring responsibilities are leaving academia. Despite the posturing of radicalism within universities and the general perception of liberalism in academic environments, equal opportunities initiatives have been slow to take hold, and the consequent reality is that the major losers in academia are women with childcare responsibilities.

Bittersweet Ingredients

A dim look into the hazy stereotypical image of an academic may for many conjure up a studious, bespectacled male, nose currently attached to theoretical texts and working late into the night writing or undertaking research (children's cartoons of Professors still represent them as such!). Such lives could hardly be led concurrently with attending to the needs of children, especially the under-teens. Similarly to many professions, academia's history is based on the supported lifestyle of white, male professionals. Although lecturing is the primary task of academics, academic careers have always been built on personal profiles derived from research, writing and publication. Until a certain level in the hierarchy is reached, such activity by necessity can only take place outside of lecturing time, unless sabbaticals are secured. Securing sabbaticals usually requires staff securing funding to buy themselves out of lecturing time and ironically funding is easier to obtain if a track record of research and publication can be evidenced.

Although professorial careers (white, male, supported) have been built on the academia as lifestyle approach, this major emphasis on production has only really taken hold in the last decade. It is arguable that this tradition has been reinforced by the 1990s managerialist culture of ranking and funding individual institutions by the size and quantity of research grants held and the number of publications that academics produce. To fulfil such criteria, academia becomes a lifestyle, building on a strong tradition already, where more than most jobs (certainly any I have been in) academics are expected to be engaged constantly in reading, researching, writing and publishing in a manner that blurs the boundaries between life inside and out-side the ivory tower — but only in one way.

Lifestyle culture within academia, markedly differentiates academia from most other work settings and deconstructs the boundary between work and home. It is not uncommon to be expected to be engaged continually in research or academic reading, nor uncommon for calls to be at weekends and evenings — work may impinge on home in a way that is uncommon in other settings, but home must not impinge on work. An example that illustrates this tension occurred during the process of writing the WHEN Conference paper

> I ironically wrote the original paper in circumstances that synthesise the experi-ence I am describing above. My 6-year-old daughter had flu — she wanted me to be with her — my schedule that week (because I had blocked some days out to write), made it possible for me to work from home. Work from home with a child!! I did, of course, write after she had fallen asleep, having read some of the articles, whilst rubbing her head, trying to filter out the noise from Sesame Street whilst I did so. I wanted to and needed to write but I also wanted and needed to be with my daughter.

The expression of this tension is particularly difficult it seems in academia. Higher education is a public institution that rejects the personal and subjective as academ-ically valid because of the way it constructs its particular form of knowledge. Academia both as an institution and in its writing marginalizes and devalues emo-tions (Ribbens, 1994). Interestingly, research also documents that whilst presenting hostility to the spill over of the private into the public (although expecting and legitimizing the opposite), expectations based on sexist stereotypes of women's caring skills have been capitalized on by expecting women to take on a large part of pastoral care of students either formally or by default, because attention has not been given to the needs of students in these areas (West and Lyon, 1995).

Feminists (Spender, 1983 and 1985; Stanley and Wise, 1983) have argued that within higher education institutions there is a separation of formal educational knowledge and the knowledge acquired through living. As Edward's (1993) states

> Public, objective, institutional and pedagogic epistemologies are given validity over and above private, subjective, emotional and personal ways of knowing — even when the former can be viewed to have arisen from a white patriarchal knowledge, norms, values and strictures.

As David et al. (1993), have noted academia does not accord well with feminists' way of working, which are about collaboration and the dismantling of hierarchies. In terms of building an academic career, a set of expectations have developed from the organizational culture (values, beliefs, traditions and practices), which although problematic for many academics, particularly women and disabled academics (see French this volume), have a very particular effect for those with caring responsibil-ities. The overriding features of academic culture are its individualism, competitive-ness and hierarchy.

Academic success is primarily judged by individual success, both in terms of an individual's career and the RAE (Research Assessment Exercise) upon which a large proportion of the university's funding is based. I and others have been reminded that joint publications are not given as much credibility as sole or first authorship. For parents, there is limited time outside of their lecturing or research commitments to undertake their own research and writing. This can be a major obstacle — it can be infinitely more feasible and possible to undertake collaborative projects with others — yet seemingly these achievements are regarded as somehow of less value.

Given that this is the overarching context in which we work, it is arguable that such an environment, more than most, creates a culture in which the expression of the tensions and emotions raised at times by role conflict of parenting and working, is deemed more unacceptable than in other settings. This can be particularly power-ful when coupled with the pervasive assumption that being an academic requires staff to be permanently and therefore exclusively engaged and interested in aca-demic pursuits. This tacitly expected level of commitment, may be undesirable for many, but is simply not possible for those who are actively engaged in caring commitments.

The literature reviewed in the next section, indicates that women with caring responsibilities are not doing as well as their peers in terms of the criteria by which academic success is judged. Whilst we may and should take issue with those criteria, it is of concern that women with children appear to be disadvantaged in terms of building an academic career. However, one of the issues raised by the lack of research data in this area, is that although there are indications that women with children are leaving academia, we do not know the proportion of these compared with the number who stay, because in the UK we do not know how many academics are also parents. There is an indication in the literature that women in particular cover up their private lives to retain their professional credibility. Leonard and Malina (1994) emphasize in the discussions of their research the hidden presence of motherhood — the lack of any recognition or reference to people's private respons-ibilities and pleasures in the family context. Being a mother, they conclude, is a predominately silent experience, what Hoschild (1989) terms the cultural cover up where any traces of stress or need for compromise are kept underground (Aisenberg and Harrington, 1988). Academic women, they conclude, can thus be seen to be struggling to perform within the traditional male model of having someone at home, quietly erasing the problems caused by childraising responsibilities.

In the States, the consequences of this system appear to be that women are leaving universities to pursue their discipline in industrial or statutory settings. Wilson's (1995) article reflects the feeling amongst some academics that you still have to choose whether to be an academic with tenure, in which case you don't have children or have them and face the reality of losing your career — this is gender specific, as one women who left stated:

> Being a Professor is not a 40-hour week job . . . it's designed for either single people or males whose wives stay home and take care of everything.

As long ago as 1964, Jessie Bernard wrote that as many as one fourth of the women who earn PhDs drop out of their professions, permanently or temporarily, to rear families. Koller Finkel et al. state that in 1994 the position was little different and many women have had to leave academia or settle for positions on the periphery.

This resonates with the experience of women in Britain. AUT researchers discovered that once women leave to have children they almost never return to academic work and virtually no women resign academic posts and then return when children are at school age (Day, 1986). For individuals this is demotivating and demoralizing. For academia generally, this is an enormous waste of skills and talent.

Shaking the Cocktail — Women, Motherhood and Academic Careers

Although there is a growing, and needed literature on gender and education (Davies, Lubelska and Quinn, 1994; Walsh and Morley, 1995), from which it is clear that women are still not achieving equality with men in terms of holding senior posts, attracting grants nor in the level of publications, little attention has been given to the specific issue of motherhood and academia.

When discussing the career paths of women, most authors do not address the differences which child-bearing might make for women. Leonard and Malina's 1994 work is the only UK reference I could find that explicitly puts the two together. At an unnamed university, that has an extensive Social Sciences resource, a reference search on motherhood and academia returned the response — nil subject area!! The primary source of information is therefore North American.

In Leonard and Malina's study of motherhood and academia they noted that

> the task of combining motherhood with the demands of academic life is a difficult one — a fact that is reflected in the relative rarity of mothers occupying full-time academic posts.

For those women with children who are in academia, reaching the benchmarks now defined as a measure of academic success, that is, publication, attracting research grants, the odds are not good. Stiver Lie (1990) suggests that women's publication rates are negatively correlated with the period during which they have children under 10 years old. In her study of women faculty, Nancy Whitley (1987), found that the women had fewer publications and fewer grants than their male peers, Whitley suggests that women lag behind men in productivity because women bear children and assume responsibility for their care. Nancy Hensel, examining the productivity of women faculty, concludes in most cases, the presence of children serves as a deterrent to women's publishing efforts (1990).

In America, two recent articles reflect the similarities in situations faced by academic mothers, which is compounded by the tenure rules that operate. Wilson (1995) states that a generation after women regularly began mixing motherhood with careers, female academics are still struggling with the combination. Their predicament is still more complicated than usual, they say, because the tenure clock coincides directly with the biological clock. In the United States there is not only pressure to publish regularly, but your employment status depends on it. This pressure can be felt particularly acutely by women who both want to have children during the course of their pre-tenure period and mothers who are less able to commit the additional time required over and above a teaching day to pursuing their own research and writing for publication. Less than two years ago, a female biologist won tenure at Vassar College after a federal judge found the institution had denied her promotion because she was married and a mother (Wilson, 1995). In Finkel et al.'s (1994) review of childbirth, tenure and promotion, it is concluded that there is a

> glaring disparity between what faculty believe and what faculty do concerning the critical issue of care for infants (sic). The implications of parenthood on work productivity is minimally recognised in policy and ignored by many in practice.

Although many universities in America do now have policies allowing parents to stop the tenure clock temporarily, many are reluctant to take the extra time, still feeling it will count against them and similarly to the UK, the more powerful, informal culture still prevails. Finkel states that to make a change in the number of women who ultimately reach the senior academic levels, institutions of higher education must recognize that an increasing number of junior faculty women will want to bear children and rear them. These women should not be denied the opportunity to progress in academia because they have decided to have a family while pursuing their careers.

It would appear that an academic lifestyle affects women's wider relationships. Simeone's (1987) research indicated that compared to men, academic women are more likely to be never married, to report less stable marriages (sic), be divorced, have fewer children and to see children as a detriment to their careers. Similarly, Blackstone and Fulton's (1975) study indicated that many women in academia have chosen to remain without partners and children. For those academic women who are in partnerships, they are more likely to be working or studying part-time, to hold lower ranks, and eventually to be unemployed or in jobs unrelated to their training.

Whilst this previous research can be criticized for its over-preoccupation with marriage and heterosexual partnerships, rather than looking at the diverse range of relationships and personal lifestyle women may be committed to, the research does suggest the difficulty involved for women in combining parental and other relationships with the lifestyle expected of academics. This resonates with Edwards's study of mature women students and the notion that educational establishments and home life are in tension with one another, particularly in relation to the value given to academia (public life) over home life (private life). Clearly missing from both the studies on mature mother students and academic mothers are the perspectives of lesbian mothers, single mothers, those with several children and male carers.

61

The dominant discourse in the literature reviewed above is about research and particularly publication. Academic success is equated with productivity in these fields and how to compensate women who don't produce enough, particularly because of their caring responsibilities. It is important to question how and by whom this profile of a successful academic has been constructed, and for whom? The literature reviewed above suggests that the dominant conception of what it is to be an academic is particularly difficult to fulfil for women with children. There are many other ways in which achieving academic success could be measured — for example, what about quality of teaching? What about a wider definition and validation of other forms of research, for example, action research? What about collaborative work and other, and often more relevant, ways of disseminating material other than through refereed texts? This is a broader issue of concern I know to women and men, with or without children, but has a particular significance for the former group.

Clearly, the dissemination of ideas and research findings is important. The pertinent question in the current culture is about who gets to construct debates and disseminate ideas. It is critical that women, including women with children, are part of this.

Drinking the Cocktail — Intoxication and Aftertaste (the Hidden Kick)

These issues derive from the culture of academia but this clearly has implications for how these conflicts are played out between staff members. Such an environment can provide scope for support between women but it can also lead to ambivalence and conflict as some of these experiential examples illustrates.

My major advocates have been other women in academia, whose sharing and understanding of my experiences have evoked immeasurable support. When I became pregnant in the middle of a two-year part-time MA, the head of department at my college invested considerable personal time in encouraging me to go back to the course without intermitting, since she had noticed with concern the propensity for women to intermit in similar circumstances and not return. More than this, she facilitated an infrastructure to enable me to attend lectures and seminars. My PhD supervisor acknowledged unprovoked in our first session together, the additional responsibilities that I have and her need to be flexible and considerate in relation to that. I can't tell you what a relief it was when she stated 'I know what it's like, I raised four myself'. I am very aware that these examples are from personal commitments. It was not something built into the structures, nor even debated in the college but was reliant on the individuals concerned. This experience stands in light relief to the experience of another colleague, whose male tutor, a well known radical in his area and a father himself, refused to mark her work which was late because her child had been ill and whose reaction to her pregnancy part way through her PhD was that she was doing it the hard way.

However, the criteria for academic success can create tensions between women. One colleague was told by another feminist academic that the university she had chosen to study her PhD at, which was in her home town, where she has two young children at school, was unlikely to consider her application for an academic post because the university preferred to encourage fresh blood. She was also advised to spend the first few years of her academic career moving on and experiencing a wide range of settings. Who could fulfil this criteria and be the fresh blood this apparently radical university was seeking? Certainly very few parents would be in a position to frequently move themselves and their families around the country in order to obtain the required experience.

Such an environment and the feelings it engenders can provoke overreactions. I felt this recently when invited to attend a meeting (all female) at 8.30 am — two hours from home on a school holiday! In every other circumstance the women in that group and I would share similar views and experiences and act as a great support for one another, but our differences this time in relation to parenting, held the potential to divide us. These incidents exaggerate the divisions in experience, from peers who do not have children. This means that tensions, concerns and conflicts do not get expressed. A particularly sad incident was of a colleague who belatedly spoke of her children and who confided that she would never talk of them at work or display their pictures because of the way in which she had observed this acting to other women's detriment they (male and female academics) just won't take you seriously.

This tension between women was confirmed in the WHEN workshop, when the ideas in this paper were first presented. It was also persuasively pointed out in the workshop that this silence on experience is felt acutely by feminists who are involuntarily childless and whose experience, particularly of fertility treatment, can potentially isolate them from feminists with children and those who have consciously chosen not to have them.

There is the additional complication of initiatives that in theory broaden educational opportunities to women students with children but which may set staff and student interests in conflict. Another colleague, also a mother and academic, recently received a job description that required evening work in line with the college's expanding extra-curricular programme. She felt unable to apply for such a post, knowing that both arranging childcare would be a problem and because she did not want to leave her children at night as well as during the day. The irony is that potentially this college's evening programme may be opening doors for mature female students and may be the only time some mothers can attend educational classes. This highlights the tensions that may arise between women with otherwise common interests.

To manage their role conflict many women choose to work part-time. However, there is in academia a prevalent ambivalence and hostility to part-timers (many of whom are women and mothers) who are treated as less than serious academics. The workload of many part-timers, particularly lecturers, prohibits them from researching and publishing — the criteria on which it seems most promotions are based, rather than the quality of their teaching.

Although we do not (yet?) have such a pressured tenure system as that in America, it is of interest that increasingly lecturing and research posts are being offered on fixed term contracts. I, like others, feel a pressure to conform to a publication record set by those without parenting responsibilities and a dilemma in relation to having more children — I feel unable to take the risk that my contract will not be extended if I either get pregnant or fail to produce the required outputs. The first marks a division between myself and male colleagues who will never have to face this issue, the second puts me in unequal competition with those who can choose to spend evenings or weekends pursuing, without interruption, their personal research.

These conflicts can affect all parents, although there is a conspicuous lack of voice in the research that does exist of fathers' perspectives and dilemmas. Given the predominant imbalance in career opportunities and caring responsibilities between the genders, conflict rather than support between male and female parents is likely. One male colleague on observing my photo of my daughter, talked of his own and described her as the centre of his life. I know that this same colleague gets into work very early, leaves very late and frequently attends weekend conferences. When once I talked of the dilemma I faced when my child was ill and there was no parental leave policy at work, he explained that his partner (female) worked part-time, very flexible hours and so 'we don't have that problem'!

The absence of fathers' views and perspectives does present a problem, since this debate needs to be developed in relation to current discussions on men and masculinity, and men and parenting. Interestingly, the most current literature on re-assessing men's role and responsibilities as fathers (Burgess, 1997) does so firmly in tandem with demanding changes in organizational practices, without which a better balance between home and work is not envisaged. The focus in this chapter, however, remains on women, on mothers, since it is clear that academic organizational culture works to their detriment.

What is also clear, is that since many women with children do go back to, or start professions in other settings, it raises some fundamental questions about what it is about academic culture and organization that deters women with children from staying there. Whilst wider gender issues about the allocation of domestic responsibility of childcare within households is critical, solutions cannot be reduced to this, not least because of the variety of relationships and circumstances that mothers live in. The above discussion suggests that academic culture is largely responsible for an environment where the expression of the tensions and conflicts it induces for parents, particularly mothers, is suppressed.

Remixing the Concoction

Perhaps the emphasis on getting women into the public domain has left the critique of it largely wanting. Whilst feminist activity in this area has been critical, there is a need now to explore other ways of working and place a corresponding emphasis on the need for higher education organizations to respond to diverse circumstances.

This debate is quite well developed in the statutory sectors, (SSI, 1991) but not so articulated in academia. What is it about academia that prevents or inhibits the discourse? How does the structure and culture in academia articulate with the responsibilities of parenthood? The above examples and discussion suggest pointers, but this is a vastly under-researched area in the UK and if we are to re-mix this cocktail to make it more palatable then more action and research is needed to understand and tackle these issues. Those that may have been expected to lead the way appear to be either leaving academia or are silenced — by necessity to protect their career or by the ambivalent relationship that motherhood has to feminism. The latter may inhibit other feminists from leading work in this area.

Feminism has always had this ambivalent relationship to motherhood, seeing women's confinement to the home and within the family as central to their oppression. Whilst feminism has, importantly and significantly, critiqued and deconstructed the way in which motherhood and maternal instinct has been socially constructed (e.g. Ribbens, 1994; David et al., 1993), what has had considerably less emphasis and understanding is the recognition of the emotional context and dynamic of the relationship and the significance that women attribute to its experience (Freely, 1995). Whilst our construction of our experience is problematic and we cannot hope to be immune from internalized patriarchal definitions surrounding women and motherhood, to negate or marginalize the importance of mothering to women does us an injustice. bell hooks, an African-American feminist has argued passionately that motherhood is not just central to the experience of black women but far preferable to the degrading and dehumanizing work they have had to do from slavery to the present. Motherhood is an understandably difficult subject for feminists to re-explore but an essential one in developing feminist theorizing.

It is crucial therefore to give voice to the diversity of feelings and dilemmas that feminist mothers in academia face. Parents exist in a multitude of forms and many women choose and want to have children. This should not lead to their exclusion from their chosen careers; it certainly has not for their male counterparts.

Conclusion

The very tensions that motherhood highlights and its emotive expression strike deep at the core and tradition of academia. Academic culture with its emphasis on the cerebral, on logic and rationality, is a resistant bastion to such expression. Given the gendered connotation of such characteristics it is important feminists challenge rather than collude with this culture. The starting point and crux of my original paper was experiential. It was an exploration of ideas and issues that have arisen from my own experiences in academia in relation to the relationships and responsibilities I have as a mother. This affords the advantages of a challenge to theory (or lack of it), based on lived experience and the problems associated with experiential knowledge i.e. it is inevitably partial, most significantly, as a white woman, with one child, I am not intending to, nor could I generalize from my own experience to adequately encompass that of others, but I am concerned by the paucity of research in this area and want my experience to inform and further the debate.[1]

An important sub-theme of this chapter is the relationship between knowing, knowledge and theory. Academic knowledge has been powerfully critiqued by feminists (Gunew, 1990; Edwards, 1993) who have exposed the marginalization or exclusion of women from academia's objective knowledge base, in terms of both methodology and access. This knowledge base has then been used to further reinforce prescribed roles and attributes for women, based on the apparent truths of the data. Theory based on experential knowledge was the starting point for second wave feminism, establishing the principle that collective experience could form the basis for feminist knowledge and theory. Experiential knowledge based in the local and particular has been and will inevitably remain in tension with the conceptually ordered framework of academia (Edwards, 1993). It is a problematic but critical reference point for the development of feminist knowledge, bringing with it the challenges and potential of commonality of women's experience and its diversity based on race, class, age, sexual orientation and perhaps parenting status.

Central to different feminist approaches is the critique of the divide between the public and the private — being an academic and a mother provides a pertinent example of the dialectic and the need for integration in order for women to do more than superficially occupy jobs and participate in the public world. Currently women may feel forced to make decisions based on a male modelled career pattern. It is not just about women coming up with complex coping strategies for dealing with this situation (although they may need to do this concurrently) it is also about institutions responding and initiating change. It is not enough to confine the debate to the private and to focus it on male/female relations there. Such debates embody heterosexual assumptions anyway and obscure the issues for lesbian parents. It is not only about shared responsibility for childcare. It is more than this. It is about the recognition and responsiveness of organizations to parents' needs — institutions have diverse employees and they should recognize diverse needs and not reinforce the model, appropriate only to single people and derived from single or supported males.

Whilst the challenge of gender relations at home will continue to be an important area of activity for many women, resolutions in this area will not affect the need to transform organizational culture based on patriarchal norms and values. The right to be successful at work, in academia, ought not to foreclose possibilities to female members of staff or their commitment to parenting. Currently women are still marginalized in academic institutions. Mothers are marginalized still further.

Note

1   Particular thanks go to: LesleyAnne Ezelle, Senior Research Fellow, Anglia Polytechnic University.

References

AISENBERG, N. and HARRINGTON, M. (1988) *Women of Academe: Outsiders in the Sacred Grove*, Amherst: University of Massachusetts Press.

BERNARD, J. (1964) *Academic Women*, University Park: The Pennsylvania State University Press.

BLACKSTONE, T. and FULTON, O. (1975) 'Sex discrimination among university teachers — A British American comparison', *British Journal of Sociology*, **26**, pp. 261–75.

BURGESS, A. (1997) *Fatherhood Reclaimed,* London: Vermilion.

DAVID, M., EDWARDS, R., HUGHES, M. and RIBBENS, J. (eds) (1993) *Mothers and Education: Inside Out?*, Basingstoke: Macmillan.

DAVIES, S., LUBELSKA, C. and QUINN, J. (1994) *Changing the Subject: Women in Higher Education*, London: Taylor and Francis.

DAY, T. (1986) AUT Woman, *AUT bulletin*, **9**, Autumn, London.

EDWARDS, R. (1993) *Mature Women Students: Separating or Connecting Family and Education*, London: Taylor and Francis.

FREELY, M. (1995) 'Keeping mum in everywoman', *What about Us? An Open Letter to the Mothers Feminism Forgot*, London: Bloomsbury, pp. 10–12.

GUNEW, S. (ed.) (1990) *Feminist Knowledge: Critique and Construct*, London: Routledge.

HENSEL, N. (1990) 'Maternity, promotion and tenure: Are they compatible?', in WELCH, L. (ed.) *Women in Higher Education: Changes and Challenges*, New York: Praeger.

HOSCHILD, A.R. (1989) *The Second Shift: Working Parents and the Revolution at Home*, London: Piaktus.

KOLLER FINKEL, S., OLSWANG, S. and SHE, N. (1994) 'Childbirth, tenure, and promotion', *The Review of Higher Education*, Spring, **17**, 3, pp. 259–70.

LEONARD, P. and MALINA, D. (1994) 'Caught between two worlds: Mothers as academics', in DAVIES, S. et al. *Changing the Subject: Women in Higher Education*, London: Taylor and Francis, pp. 29–41.

MORLEY, L. (1994) 'Glass ceiling or iron cage: Women in UK academia', *Gender, Work and Organisation*, **1**, 4, pp. 194–204.

RIBBENS, J. (1994) *Mothers and Their Children: A Feminist Sociology of Childrearing,* London: Sage.

RICH, A. (1977) *Of Women Born: Motherhood as Experience and Institution*, London: Virago.

SIMEONE, A. (1987) *Academic Women: Working Towards Equality*, South Hadley, MA: Bergin and Garvey.

SPENDER, D. (1983) 'Theorising about theorising', in BOWLES, G. and DUELLI KLEIN, R. (eds) *Theories of Women's Studies*, London: Routledge and Kegan Paul.

SPENDER, D. (1985) *For the Record: The Making and Meaning of Feminist Knowledge*, London: The Women's Press.

SSI (1991) *Women in Social Services: A Neglected Resource,* London: HMSO.

STANLEY, L. and WISE, S. (1983) *Breaking Out: Feminist Consciousness and Feminist Research*, London: Routledge and Kegan Paul.

STIVER LIE, S. (1990) 'The juggling act: Work and family in Norway', in STIVER LIE, S. and O'LEARY, V.E. *Storming the Tower: Women in the Academic World*, London: Kogan Page.

WALSH, V. and MORLEY, L. (eds) (1995) *Breaking Boundaries: Women in Higher Education*, London: Taylor and Francis.

WEST, J. and LYON, K. (1995) 'The trouble with equal opportunities: The case of women academics', *Gender and Education*, **7**, 1, pp. 51–68.

WHILEY, N. (1987) 'Women in academic radiology', *American Journal of Radiology*, **149**, pp. 438–9.

WILKINSON, S. and KITZINGER, C. (1993) *Heterosexuality: A Feminism and Psychology Reader,* London: Sage.

WILSON, R. (1995) 'Scheduling motherhood', *The Chronicle of Higher Education*, 10 March, pp. 14–15.

6 'All in a Day's Work': Gendered Care Work in Higher Education

Tina Barnes-Powell and Gayle Letherby

Introduction

In this chapter we are going to explore the gendered nature of 'care work' within higher education. As Cotterill and Waterhouse in this volume note, 'care' is a gendered concept. Both in the wider community and in the communities of higher education (whether provided by women or men), 'care' is feminized and undervalued.

It is well known that horizontal and vertical gender segregation exists in academe (Evetts, 1994). As Bagilhole (1994) notes in both the 'new' and 'old' universities, women academics remain in a very small minority representing only 20 per cent of full-time staff. Further to this, according to the figures available for 'new' universities while 30 per cent of lectures are women, this falls to 10 per cent or less for grades above Senior Lecturer.

Firstly, we will introduce biographical accounts of our experiences as lecturers. These are concerned specifically with our relationship to students we taught, who were predominantly women. Secondly, we will discuss the ways in which our experiences highlight important issues and concerns for women academics working within higher education, such as the gendered nature of women's roles within the university, and the ways in which our access to spaces in the university is often restricted and controlled by the demands of the 'care work' that women become involved in.

Biographical Accounts

It is important to note, that for both of us it was our first year of full-time teaching. We were both appointed in fairly junior positions in the Social Sciences division at a new university, and we each had a large teaching load and substantial administrative duties, which entailed large amounts of paperwork and student contact. We were also both trying to finish our doctorates.

Gayle's Biographical Account

My main teaching responsibilities lay in sociology with some teaching on the women's studies part of the University's Applied Social Science (ASS) degree. In terms of administrative duties my role was that of Project Tutor and joint Third Year Adviser to students on the ASS degree. In practical terms my job as Project Tutor involved organization of the third year double module which all ASS students had to take to achieve an honours' degree. This involved allocating students to supervisors, coordinating-ordinating module timetables, marking and dealing with students' general problems related to the module. In my role as adviser I was again a point of contact for third year students if they had personal or academic worries, of if they needed coursework extensions. I shared this job with the male Sociology Subject Group Head.

Early in the first week of the autumn term I had a meeting with the third year students to outline the project module requirements to them. On advice from course tutors and subject leaders I had set the first deadline for the end of the following week. For this deadline students had to pick a subject for research, decide broadly on their methodological approach and if possible write a paragraph in relation to their substantive and methodological intentions. Following consultation with subject leaders (in sociology, social policy and psychology) I was to allocate each student a supervisor. At the meeting and all the following week, students complained to me about the short notice they had been given. Despite this, most of the proposals came in on time and supervisors were allocated. Following this, students began to grumble to me about the next deadline which required a more detailed outline proposal and the completion of an ethics form as each project had to be approved internally by the School's Ethics Committee. The ethics committee and the introduction of a detailed proposal were new school-driven aspects of the module, yet students complained to me that it was unfair of me to make them do this, when students in previous years had not had to.

Towards the end of November, as things were beginning to settle down, I returned to my office after a lecture to find several third year students waiting for me. One student (who I'll call Ann), stepped forward and said (fairly loudly and it appeared angrily) that she had a problem. Briefly, Ann had changed her supervisor without consulting me and had now decided that she wanted to change back. However, in the meantime her original supervisor (Tina in fact) had been allocated another student. Ann talked 'at me' very loudly for a couple of minutes, accusing me of giving her an inappropriate supervisor. I explained that the change had been her own choice and that her original supervisor was not now available. After further protest from Ann I added that my job was administrative and if she wanted to change I would have to talk to the Subject Group Head. Ann then stepped close to me so that her face was just inches away from mine and shouted 'you do that then'. I was extremely distressed by this for several days.

My other academic responsibility did not appear particularly onerous until the spring term. Towards the end of January I started to have visits from lots of students requiring extensions, and this was quickly followed by students wanting to talk about dropping modules, and delaying taking their exams. (At this time I also moved into an office with Tina and thus started to answer similar questions from women's studies students). Later in the year I talked to my subject group head about why I saw so many more students than him. He said that he thought that it was likely that the women students in the third year (72 out of 74) came to me more specifically if their problems were 'personal' and generally because, as a woman, I was 'naturally' considered to be more approachable. To this I added that I thought as a woman in a junior position, rather than a man in a fairly senior position, I was also much easier to shout at and demand from. Although there were many students who were always polite and friendly, there were several others who complained verbally and on paper that I was never available and got angry with me. I couldn't 'deliver' what they wanted.

At the end of the summer term I was already dreading the new academic year. But things did get better, for example when the students returned in October, several of them greeted me. Furthermore, the management of the project module was easier, as I organized a meeting for the third years the previous May, and although in relation to this module and the third year in general, students were not a problem, I found things easier. Despite improvements though, I still felt and feel that the students expect me and other staff (especially the women) to be there for them above all else. The week before I wrote this personal account one student referred to my life as similar to that of 'Riley's', when I told her that I couldn't meet her the next day as I had a meeting.

Tina's Biographical Account

Prior to being appointed as a lecturer I worked in a Community Drugs Team. My brief was to work with professionals and young people as a drugs trainer and educator. But after seven and a half years of daily exposure to the desperate and often hopeless circumstances in which young people were living, I needed a change. I decided to enter higher education to teach women's studies. My expectations were, therefore, that I would no longer be expected to deal with the complex personal problems of individuals. I believed that I was being employed 'to teach' and 'to conduct research'. I was wrong.

Teaching subjects such as domestic violence, child-abuse, pornography and addictions to male and female students on women's studies modules proved to be very challenging indeed. This meant that during my first term I found myself coping with: two disclosures of child abuse; two eating disorders; one tranquilliser dependency; four cases of domestic violence; one amphetamine dependency and two sexuality crises.

In each of these cases I tried to get the students to consult the student counselling services. In some cases I was successful, but even then, the students continued to return to me to provide progress reports. They also relied on me to fill in their student records; they did not want to speak to other members of staff about their problems, but did want them alerted to the fact that they were experiencing personal problems. I was expected, therefore, to provide this additional guidance and support, in addition to supporting a wide range of other students who were experiencing more general problems that were affecting their academic work.

To gain access to our office space the students had a variety of strategies:

1   A loud knock on the door.
2   30 seconds later, knock louder, while opening the door to gain entry.
3   Speak loudly to which ever one of us was not on the telephone (the students saw Gayle and I as interchangeable — whoever was there was spoken to, the students paid no attention to our very distinct and separate areas of responsibility).
4   If we were already occupied seeing another student the students would tell us that they needed to see us urgently, then they would wait outside the door.
5   If we were working at our desks, we were perceived to be 'free', so the students began telling us about their problems, ignoring the tasks that we were involved in.
6   On the occasions when we asked the students to book an appointment, they would tell us that their problems were really important and would not take a minute. . . . they invariably stayed until they had told their tale.

This notion that we were always available was not confined to the space of our office. We discovered that students would present us with their problems in a variety of locations: walking between lectures; in the library; in the car park; in a café while at lunch; even in the toilet! On several occasions we tried locking our office door. The students' response was to knock the door, knock the door again much more loudly while trying to open the door, then wait outside the door until we allowed them in.

It was as though we were not allowed any type of personal space. Normally, I am used to a range of different personal spaces according to my type of interaction. While at work I expect my interactions to be dictated by the conventions of 'social distance' or 'public distance' (Henley, 1977). Yet frequently students assumed personal or intimate distance with me in wholly inappropriate locations. When students sat beside me in the library or in a nearby café, or stood beside me while I was washing my hands in the toilet, they were not observing any notions of 'proper distances' (Goffman, 1963). Prior to working in higher education I had felt that my teacher/student interactions were generally under my control. It was only in exceptional circumstances that I felt unable to negotiate a satisfactory teacher–student relationship. Yet within the university I felt that there was nowhere where I could go to escape from being 'on tap' to the continual demands of the students. Even on the very rare occasions that Gayle and I were able to get away for a half hour break, we would invariably return to our office to find queues of students enquiring where we had been because they had been trying to find us!

All of these examples demonstrate the ways in which the less powerful were managing their resources very effectively, thus exerting their control over us — the supposedly more powerful teaching staff. On several occasions students told both Gayle and I that they were the 'customers', and they had 'rights'. These rights extended as far as shouting at us if things were not going very smoothly, demanding to know where we were if we weren't readily available in our offices, and asking us for appointments on days they knew should be our 'research days' or our annual leave.

Power and Empowerment; Differences between Women

As Bhopal (1994, p. 130) argues the 'language of academia is white, middle class and male'. Despite our disadvantages by virtue of our sex (see for example the following section), as two white women lecturers we recognize that we are in a privileged position in relation to women in general, and our women students in particular. As Bhopal adds, 'women are a heterogenous group divided by class, race and ethnicity, by nationality and religion by age and sexual preference . . .' (1994, p. 135). These differences equate with different experience of exclusion and oppression. Thus by virtue of biological, social and material differences, many of our women students have in general less privileged lives than ourselves.

They are also less powerful in terms of the academic experience. We hold the objective balance of power in that we have control over the material and authoritative resources (Giddens, 1985). We have the power to give or not to give extensions to students. It is us and not them that assess and grade student work and that speak up (or not) for students at Exam Boards. Thus: 'the notion of power . . . remains inextricably connected to real inequalities in material and social circumstances' (Kramarae and Treichler, 1985, p. 351). Yet it is important to note that within relationships power is not fixed. As Worsley (1973) argues 'power does not exist "in itself"; it flows between people. And everybody has some of it, some area of choice, of ability to affect things his (sic) way' (Worsley, 1973, p. 250). Power is never a simple matter of 'haves' and 'have nots'. Any investigation of power will, therefore, also uncover the 'dialectic of control' (Giddens, 1985, p. 374).

Yet our biographical accounts have demonstrated that the subjective experience of power in university life is often ambivalent for the lecturer as well as for the student. Indeed, we have shown how the less powerful 'manage' resources very effectively to exert control over the more powerful in establishing their relationships in higher education.

As students, we each felt empowered by our educational experience. So as feminists beginning our first full time academic post, we hoped that we could facilitate similar personal development in other women. In some ways, whilst writing this paper, we have begun to appreciate that our experiences actually demonstrate that we are in part achieving what we set out to do. Recently a student told Gayle that her women friends felt able to criticize the university, the degree, the modules and the tutors, because their experience of education had empowered them to do so, and as Davies et al. (1994, p. 10) argue:

> empowerment for women in Higher Education is seen to be about us, as women doing it for ourselves, as activists and subjects, aware of the political as well as educational implications of our actions.

Like Owen (1994, p. 96), we have both found working with women students in a women's studies context 'stimulating and enjoyable'. Furthermore, our students have spoken positively about our teaching styles and the content of the lectures and seminars that we deliver. This is both pleasing and rewarding. It suggests that the students feel that they can make comments to us about our teaching. It also suggests that the students are happy about the educational experience we are providing.

Hierarchies of Hardship; or Ontological Similarities

In this new university, institutional directives often made or make life difficult for the students. They have a heavy workload: eight modules which run over three terms each year with two pieces of assessed work for each module. Many students need a lot of academic, as well as personal support. This is particularly relevant for women students, if we accept (which we do) that universities are patriarchal institutions with patriarchal ways of thinking (Owen, 1994). Or, as the Hansard Report 1990 noted, 'bastions of male power and privilege'. As our biographical accounts have shown, our students often expect us to provide 'care work' or support for them instantly. It is clear that on the one hand our students see us as approachable, accessible and understanding. They attach to us the role as 'carer', because they expect us to be more understanding than some of the male lecturers. As a result they also often see us as separate from the dominant patriarchal culture. On the other hand, when students find the institution oppressive, they see us as contributing to, and responsible for, the system. It is in these circumstances that the students see their oppression as partly our fault.

In accounting for this, we would argue that it is necessary to take account of New Right policy, theory and common sense, which as Epstein (1995) argues has since the 1980s become the dominant cultural discourse. As Epstein adds, a key issue for the New Right has been the marketization of public services:

> The Higher Education sector is increasingly being forced into, and, in some cases has willingly adopted the entrepreneurial spirit of the market. One consequence of the move toward entrepreneurialism which most of us are experiencing is a shift towards the stronger 'managerial' culture in higher education. (Epstein, 1995, pp. 59–60)

In response to this:

> students enter ... with beliefs in their entitlement to judge provision (be it by feminist and/or consumerist criterion). They also speak a language of commodification. The investments they have made — both economic and personal — generate a desperation for an education which will produce success ... (Skeggs, 1994, p. 7)

The success of New Right ideology is clear, as it is not just the younger students ('Thatcher's Children') who refer to their 'consumer rights', but older students also. From our experience we would suggest that older mature students can be as demanding as the younger student cohort. By drawing on stereotypes of women as nurturers, the institution (and many students) assume that women lecturers will be the main providers of 'care work'. The institution also expects us to teach, to do 'our share' of administration and to do research and publish. As individuals and as members of academic institutions, we are expected to accept the 'success ethic', working for high research ratings and excellence in teaching (see Evans, 1990). Also, as feminists, we find that on top of all of these 'tasks' we also have to defend our politics, our perspective and sometimes our students. As Culley et al. (1985) notes:

> ... as mothers, we are expected to nurture; as professionals we are expected to compete. The context in which our nurturing is to take place is in the patriarchal context in which we teach. ... In our culture the role of the nurturer and intellectual have been separated not just by gender, but by function; to try to combine them is to create confusion. (Culley et al., 1985, p. 12)

Students sometimes don't recognize, and on occasions deny the pressures that we feel we are under. When we were students, we too understood little of what academics actually did. But we were aware that the women academics were different from most of the men. We could also see that the women academics were absent from the university cafeteria and pub cultures that the male staff appeared to be part of. We realized this because we were women first, students second. Stanley (1991) suggests that:

> ... there is a common external material reality that all women face, characterised by inequality, exploitation and oppression; and it exists precisely because we are women and not men. (Stanley, 1991, p. 207)

Our students did not seem to appreciate that, although there were very real differences between us, we should be trying to work together.

Brief Reflections

We have argued that 'care work' within academic institutions is gendered. Due to political changes, both materially and culturally, many students expect/demand more support from academic staff than has previously been the case. We suggest that students attending university in the 1990s actually need more support than has been given in the past. In the new universities in particular, students have been accepted onto degree courses who find it difficult to cope with the academic demands of university life. Often these students have been accepted into departments where academics have been told that they must publish to increase their research outputs. It is therefore inevitable that relationships between students and lecturers will sometimes be strained.

Having said this, we have felt and do feel supported by many of the students that we teach. Also, many of the women and some of the men we work with support us through good times and bad. Yet we can not believe that the 'bad' experiences we have had can be unique to us. Operating as part of the institutions we work in, as well as working to assist in the development of other women, we feel that by being approachable to students we collude with the stereotype that women should be more approachable than men. At the same time, because we are part of the system, we feel that students tend to focus on our identities as academics rather than our identities as women. This we feel indicates the need for stronger support relationships within the academy, for us, for students, and between us and students, for as Breda Gray argues (1994, p. 86):

> Women in HE have to overcome the predominantly individualistic culture within the academy in order to communicate with each other and to develop social networks.

References

ABBOTT, P. and WALLACE, C. (eds) (1991) *Gender, Power and Sexuality*, London: Macmillan.

BAGILHOLE, B. (1994) 'Being different is a very different row to hoe: Survival strategies of women academics', in DAVIES, S., LUBELSKA, C. and QUINN, J. (eds) *Changing the Subject: Women in Higher Education*, London: Taylor and Francis, pp. 15–28.

BHOPAL, K. (1994) 'The influence of feminism on black women in the higher education curriculum', in DAVIES, S., LUBELSKA, C. and QUINN, J. (eds) *Changing the Subject: Women in Higher Education*, London: Taylor and Francis.

COTTERILL, P. and WATERHOUSE, R. (1996) 'Women in higher education: The gap between corporate rhetoric and the reality of experience', Presentation at WHEN Conference, Preston, March.

CULLEY, M., DIAMOND, A., EDWARDS, L., LENNOX, S. and PONTUGES, C. (1985) 'The politics of nurturance', in CULLEY, M. and PORTUGES, C. (eds) *Gendered Subjects: The Dynamics of Feminist Teaching*, London: Routledge and Kegan Paul, pp. 12–13.

DAVIES, K., LEIJENAAR, M. and OLDERSMA, J. (1991) *The Gender of Power*, London: Sage.

DAVIES, S., LUBELSKA, C. and QUINN J. (eds) (1994) *Changing the Subject: Women in Higher Education*, London: Taylor and Francis.

EPSTEIN, D. (1995) 'In our (New) Right minds: The hidden curriculum and the academy', in MORLEY, L. and WALSH, V. (eds) *Feminist Academics Creative Agents for Change*, London: Taylor and Francis.

EVANS, M. (1990) 'The problem of gender for women's studies', *Women's Studies International Forum*, **13**, 5, pp. 457–62.

EVETTS, J. (1994) *Women and Career: Themes and Issues in Advanced Industrial Societies*, London: Longman.

GIDDENS, A. (1985) *The Nation State and Violence*, Cambridge: Polity Press.

GOFFMAN, E. (1963) *Behaviour in Public Places*, Glencoe Illinois: Free Press.

GRAY, B. (1994) 'Women in higher education: What are we doing to ourselves?,' in DAVIES, S., LUBELSKA, C. and QUINN, J. (eds) *Changing the Subject: Women in Higher Education*, London: Taylor and Francis.

HANSARD SOCIETY (1990) *The Report of the Hansard Society Commission on Women at the Top*, London: Hansard Society.

HENLEY, N. (1977) *Power, Sex and Non-verbal Communication*, New York: Simon and Schuster.

KRAMARAE, C. and TREICHLER, P. (1985) *A Feminist Dictionary*, London: Pandora.

OWEN, M. (1994) 'Commonality and difference, theory and practice,' in DAVIES, S., LUBELSKA, C. and QUINN, J. (eds) *Changing the Subject: Women in Higher Education*, London: Taylor and Francis.

SKEGGS, B. (1994) 'Women's studies in Britain in the 1990s: Entitlement cultures and institutional constraints', Presentation at Women's Studies Network (UK) Conference, Portsmouth.

STANLEY, L. (1991) 'Feminist auto/biography and feminist epistemology,' in AARON, J., WALBY, S. (eds) *Out of the Margins: Women's Studies in the 1990s*, London: Falmer Press.

WORSLEY, P. (1973) 'The distribution of power in industrial society', in URRY, J. and WAKEFORD, J. (eds) *Power in Britain*, London: Heinemann.

7   Refusing to Be Typecast: The Changing Secretarial Role in Higher Education Administration

Sandra Wilkins

Introduction

The continuing development of the secretarial role in higher education administration and the general context within which changes have occurred is compared with developments in Wessex University, an 'old' university in Southern England. The functioning of academic departments only will be considered since the managerial structures and staff profiles of central administration departments closely reflect organizational hierarchies in other employment sectors.

The author is a senior secretary in an academic department, and draws upon personal experience and information gained from discussions with other secretaries. Her role as a member of a Working Group on Clerical Career Progression is the source of much of the anecdotal evidence presented here. As a negotiator for UNISON, the recognized trade union for clerical staff, member of the Equal Opportunities Committee, and Opportunity 2000 Working Group, she has been in a position to elicit the views of management on a variety of issues concerning career development. While no comparative, quantitative study has been undertaken, it is clear to the author from numerous discussions with staff from other institutions that the issues highlighted are general and widespread. Until further empirical data is available, however, the discussion that follows pertaining to Wessex University must remain an individual case study.

It is of primary concern here that important changes have taken place for secretarial staff at all levels, which remain largely unrecognized in terms of career advancement. In this context the significance of how differences in perception between secretaries and senior management influence the emphasis placed upon a need for developing strategies to improve career prospects is considered. These differences, it is suggested, evoke a minimalist approach by management to dealing with a problem which secretaries feel require more radical measures. Hence, training and personal development programmes for secretarial staff, while welcome, do little to provide real career advancement opportunities. Underlying class-based perceptions maintaining the low status ascribed to secretarial work, and attitudes generally in respect of women's traditional roles, subvert attempts to effect significant improvement (Crompton and Jones, 1984).

A major factor in maintaining obstacles impeding career progression is lack of recognition and hence value placed upon the growing complexity of tasks performed and responsibilities assumed by secretaries. Firmly entrenched attitudes are influential in determining recruitment strategies in light of a changing candidate pool for secretarial work, and in assessing staff development needs. Thus, whilst stated intentions and provision of personal development training imply active equal opportunities policies, these have little effect if real commitment to making meaningful change is absent. Crompton (1994, p. 49) observes, 'clerical and secretarial work forms the largest single category of women's employment'. Yet 'absence of any real career structure', (Coyle, 1995, p. 59) means that equal opportunities policies generally have had little impact on women in clerical posts. The nature of gendered occupations attracts little attention in terms of equality of opportunity since women here are not generally seen to be in competition with men. Further, in times of economic recession and high unemployment, equal opportunities becomes an expensive luxury and negative approaches to staffing issues are a predictable reaction.

The Changing Secretarial Role

The many important changes occurring in clerical and secretarial work during the twentieth century have provided a rich and varied source of material to sustain the interest of social commentators. Of significance has been its rapid development from an almost exclusively male to predominantly female occupation following the widespread introduction of the typewriter and telephone at the turn of the century. Concentrating on male clerical workers Lockwood (1989) noted that increasing bureaucratization and proletarianization had no significant effect on their traditional career pathways into management. Feminization of office work, on the other hand, has failed to provide women with an equivalent career structure (Crompton, 1994; Fearfull, 1996). Feminist critiques of power relationships, sexual politics and the patriarchal nature of organizations have highlighted structural and procedural barriers which impede women's career advancement (Crompton, 1994; Fearfull, 1996). Importantly, sexual harassment within the office environment has been recognized as a significant means of exercising and maintaining male power (Pringle, 1992). In higher education administration, class structures and academic elitism reinforce occupational segregation erecting further barriers to promotion opportunities between staff categories. Gender and class are thus two factors which exert significant influence on perceptions of the secretarial role, and on the need to provide adequate career development pathways.

Since the 1980s a pessimistic perspective on developments such as deskilling and further devaluing of clerical work following increased computerization has featured in discourses on organizational change (Downing, 1980; Lockwood, 1989). However, Fearfull (1996, p. 55) comments that research has been 'over-influenced by the de-skilling and degradation rhetoric' ignoring the 'range of skill development and utilization' found in clerical work. For secretaries, major changes in office procedures as a result of flatter management structures and new technology have resulted in different approaches to traditional tasks. Evidence from recruitment and training agencies, and human resource managers (Allcock, 1993; Mair and Povall, 1994; Reed Personnel, 1996) suggests that traditional secretarial skills have been enhanced and new skills acquired.

Skills acquisition is an important feature of employment patterns generally in Britain today. Gallie and White (1993, p. ix) report a 'striking rise of skill requirement of work' and a narrowing of the gap between men and women in this respect since the mid-1980s. Sixty-three per cent of workers interviewed, in a variety of occupations, believed their skills had increased over the last five years. In addition, increased skill requirement has had a marked effect upon the quality of work, job satisfaction, level of responsibility and perspectives of work in respect of demands for personal development opportunities. Whilst much of this change is attributed to computerization and technological development, Gallie and White (1993, p. 28) stress the increasing importance of 'social' and 'communication' skills. Such skills, both technical and personal, are essential to the routine administration of academic departments as service providers, although here they have yet to be accorded an equivalent level of importance.

Two other factors are influential in changing secretaries' perceptions of their role. First, a growing understanding of the particular problems facing women workers, and levels of awareness of issues concerning equality of opportunity. Second, higher levels of sophistication required in administrative and managerial abilities have motivated many secretaries to undertake additional skills and professional training, and higher education courses, increasing awareness of personal potential. Recognition of enhanced personal abilities, both traditional and recently acquired, raises career aspirations and produces higher expectations for economically active women than in the past.

In higher education administrative tasks are allocated to academic staff, usually for a preset time-scale, and according to existing teaching and research load rather than their managerial ability. In contrast, secretaries provide organizational stability and continuity: this has created opportunities for expansion and development of the secretarial role both at a personal and organizational level. Adapting traditional skills to perform an increasingly complex range of administrative and managerial functions has been critical in effecting fundamental changes. Skills such as typing and familiarity with a growing array of office equipment and computing software, are still considered essential. In addition, a survey by Tate Appointments (1995) found, secretaries frequently manage their own workloads, set goals and devise projects, supervise and train others and assume organizational or managerial control.

As secretaries recognize the value of developing and utilizing their talents and expertise, they naturally seek acknowledgment and encouragement of these pursuits by provision of genuine career advancement opportunities. However, Pringle (1992, p. 170) points to the lack of genuine career opportunities as indicating a general reluctance to acknowledge and fully understand secretarial skills, or to accept the possibility that such skills might form the base upon which to build a pathway into management. This horizontal occupational segregation, based on gender, has been well documented by theorists such as Hakim (1978) and Phillips and Taylor who maintain that 'skill definitions are saturated with sexual bias' (1980, p. 79).

Gender and the Secretarial Role

The influence that gender exerts on employers' perceptions of secretaries' career aspirations is significant. The impetus for upward mobility of men's careers assisted by assurance of long-term, continuous economic activity is rarely contested. This is bound to identification of craft skills with manhood (Phillips and Taylor, 1980, p. 85) and ideological assumptions of men as providers of a family wage (Crompton, 1994, p. 46) reinforcing patriarchal power relationships within the family as well as the workplace. These structures reflect the needs of the labour market for women, traditionally disadvantaged by low pay and low status, rather than recognizing, and acknowledging the many skills women bring to the job (Lovenduski and Randall, 1993, p. 197). Thus tensions existing between traditional expectations of the secretarial role and its increasing professionalization remain largely unrecognized. Yet Coyle (1995, p. 6) observes that '. . . patterns of gendered occupational segregation . . . remain a key factor in the entrenchment of the majority of working women in low paid, low status work'. When women do progress to higher level occupations, she adds, these are likely to be 'expertise based, rather than power based' (1995, p. 8). As a consequence secretaries moving into more senior positions often take on the role of team-leading other secretarial staff, whilst senior administrative and managerial functions continue to be dominated by male employees.

Whilst male clerical workers are expected to aspire to senior positions within organizational managerial strata, conventional assumptions are that secretaries are women who work for 'bosses' who are men (Kanter, 1977, p. 101). Problems of definition persist partly because there is no job description which will be common to all secretaries. Descriptions are often bound to stereotypical assumptions about the types of women who work as secretaries, rather than the nature of their work. Whilst 'dolly bird' has explicitly sexual connotations, 'office wife' has obvious parallels with caring and nurturing by which personal needs are met. Any power vested in a secretary is seen as merely an extension of the power of her boss, and her loyalty to him akin to the devotion expected of a wife. Activities such as hostessing strongly reaffirm her role as subordinate and oppositional to her manager in ways which reflect husband/wife or even master/servant relationship. The singular care and personal attention a manager receives from his secretary constantly re-establishes and reinforces his status.

Secretaries today reject this kind of relationship as wholly inappropriate and unprofessional. This attitude has developed as a result of feminist critiques of women's role in the labour market. Crompton sees this as indicative of 'a restructuring of the discourse of masculinity within the organisation' (1995, p. 50) perhaps representing declining patriarchal control. This reflects changing gender relationships in the workplace as equality issues become mainstream to organizational development. Emphasis has shifted from situations where secretaries work for particular individuals, to one where they work as part of a management team (Mair and Povall, 1995). The fundamental change of role from supporting to innovating and initiating change, needs to be adequately recognized and appropriately valued. This is particularly relevant in academic departments where secretaries routinely take responsibility for specific sets of tasks related to particular university procedures, for example admissions or examinations.

Traditionally secretaries are simply not expected and thus not encouraged to move outside their prescribed role and in most organizations, according to Reed Personnel (1996), occupational mobility for women between secretarial and management or administrative positions remains limited. Gaining access to the male dominated sphere of management often requires adopting an approach to work which is masculine in character. Thus, women who have been successful in breaking the 'glass ceiling' are routinely viewed as unusual and unique, rather than creating pathways which others are encouraged to follow. An underlying cause is the notion that secretaries lack the desire to change their role, an opinion not supported by an Industrial Society Report (Allcock, 1993, p. 23). From a sample of 540 secretarial and clerical workers 64 per cent of respondents expressed a wish to move from secretarial work into administrative and managerial positions. There is evidence, however, that these career ambitions remain unfulfilled. Reed Personnel (1996) found that only 7 per cent of secretaries they interviewed had achieved promotion to administrative posts. This was reported sympathetically in the *Independent* (1996), however, the media seem unable to resist using stereotypical images of secretaries. The article commented that secretaries no longer 'sit around filing their nails and typing'. Perpetuation of stereotypes such as these trivialize the role and lead to low expectations by employers and by secretaries themselves. A general decline in traditional 'male' employment opportunities has also led to an increase in the number of men who now turn to secretarial work, often as 'temps', whilst trawling the job market (Equal Opportunities Commission, 1995, p. 6). This is not surprising since the number of men who now type has risen dramatically. This is variously referred to as keyboarding, or data input, since typing remains 'women's work', though such gender differentiated language is not justified in terms of the skills involved. Men's increasing involvement in operative aspects of office work may have some impact on the way the profession is viewed, subsequently raising its status. A danger exists though, that if certain kinds of secretarial work performed by men attracts a higher status, women will be continually relegated to lesser roles, whilst male secretaries progress to the top of a new hierarchy. For as Pringle (1993) found, where secretaries are male, employers almost always assume that they will move into management. Thus male secretaries rarely encounter the barriers which prevent career advancement for women (Pringle, 1993, p. 142). The persistence of assumptions of the importance of the male breadwinner and the family wage, may be influential here.

Because of existing gender biases, concepts of masculinity, and the low value placed upon skills traditionally associated with women, male secretaries tend to hold different job titles such as Information Assistant/Officer or Administrative

Assistant and are thus relatively invisible within the secretarial workforce. The stigma attached to men working in traditionally female roles has been examined by Pringle (1993, Ch 8). This is not unique to secretarial work. Nurses who are male are almost without exception described as 'male nurses' as if their maleness needs to be established as external to their job description to differentiate them from female nurses. Undoubtedly the same rules of semantics apply to a variety of jobs undertaken by women which are traditionally viewed as male. The need to add the suffix 'ess' to certain titles, such as manageress, stewardess, authoress to distinguish the title holder as female may serve to maintain male dominance and 'ownership' of certain roles, and implies women's forays into these roles are concessionary. Such gender distinctions in job titles and functions have a continuing impact, and negative perceptions of female gendered roles persist.

The Secretarial Role in Wessex University: A Case Study

Wessex University has a predominantly female clerical population of around 700, divided into six grades. The majority of staff are located in grades 2, 3 and 4 with almost half concentrated in grade 3. Twenty per cent of staff in the top grade (6) are male. In the administrative category 45 per cent of the 160 staff are female, clustered in the lowest three grades. All heads of department in central administration are male, as are the majority of heads of academic departments.

In most organizations the management structure is 'professional' where senior administrators are likely to have educational qualifications and employment experience which equips them for management tasks. This leads to clearly defined managerial and support roles for both senior and junior administrators and the secretarial staff with whom they work. Whilst this may also be true for central administration within Wessex University, in academic departments the organizational structure is usually very different. Secretarial staff and administrators work within a hierarchy of non-professional managers — academic staff — whose tasks and duties are allocated on a rotational basis for specified timescales, usually for three years. It is likely that most academic staff have little desire to become managers and administrators — their education, training and experience have not equipped them for this role. However, administrative needs must be met and *laissez-faire* approaches to departmental management of the 1960s and 1970s have given way to budgetary devolution and decentralization. Greater emphasis is now placed upon performance indicators in terms of teaching and research output and the creation of a more competitive, market-led approach to service provision.

In this changing climate a major shift in emphasis has occurred resulting in two main effects. First, the adoption of sophisticated wordprocessing and other equipment has been crucial in modifying work patterns. Academic staff increasingly create their own documents and correspondence reducing the volume of routine typing expected of secretaries. Second, the increasing administrative load has led to the further devolution to secretarial staff. They have effectively taken on the tasks of administrators and office managers without receiving the corresponding status. Indeed, there are indications that development of new management jobs creates 'new forms of gendered labour market segregation . . . accompanied by a relative downgrading of pay and status of the management occupation' (Coyle, 1995, p. 7).

Women are generally gaining more ground in traditionally male preserves such as medicine and law, Crompton (1984) observes, and within these professions women do not experience occupational downgrading. However, in gendered occupations such as secretarial work, adaptation to different work patterns and tasks, rather than enhancing women's worth within the organization, often leads to a devaluing of the particular task involved (Crompton, 1994, p. 47). This has been a common experience for secretaries in Wessex University. UNISON has mediated for secretaries failing to gain promotion where increased responsibility has been a consequence of assuming tasks previously performed by academic staff. Once adopted, these tasks are deemed to fall within the normal definition of a particular grade.

Positive Approaches

Wessex University is beginning to respond to the need for adequate career opportunities, and is currently examining schemes which provide structured training and skills enhancement specifically designed to aid career advancement. The university has recently published its goals and aims under Opportunity 2000, one of which specifically seeks to improve career prospects for clerical staff. Opportunity 2000 is a business-led initiative designed to 'improve the quality and quantity of women's participation in the workforce' (Bargh, 1992). In addition, the Joint Negotiating Committee, which reports directly to the policy-making body concerned with staff development, is negotiating with UNISON on secretarial career development. However, to date this has concentrated upon the most senior positions affecting a mere 2 per cent of the secretarial workforce, leaving prospects for the majority unchanged.

Training and Experiential Learning

Commitment to personal development for all categories of staff has been an important feature at Wessex since 1990 when a Training and Development Unit was set up. This unit provides a wide-ranging programme of courses for secretarial staff, apart from specific skills training in word processing and computer packages. Several groups of secretaries have successfully completed 'Springboard' training — a personal development programme and networking facilitator widely used by large organizations in both the public and private sector. The Training Unit has also organized a series of seminars and workshops for women of all staff categories aspiring to future managerial roles, designed to remove the mystique surrounding management. The Training Unit provides financial support to a number of secretarial staff undertaking Open University and in-house degree programmes. Many secretaries also receive financial support, and paid time off, from their Faculties or Departments to attend skills, professional and academic courses. Accurate figures on the number of secretaries supported financially from various sources are not available, although UNISON is currently conducting a survey in this respect.

Whilst there are many advantages for secretarial staff who wish to embark upon programmes of professional training or higher education, the importance of experiential learning cannot be overlooked. Though the training opportunities provided have proved extremely valuable, they have often served to highlight the lack of specific career pathways which take account of long-term experience. Many mature women have reached senior posts in Wessex University following breaks in their career due to family responsibility, typically without the advantage of post-compulsory education. Returning to part-time, low status positions, many resume their careers at the bottom of the ladder, reaching relatively senior positions for the second time.

Secretarial staff at Wessex University are keenly aware of this problem and have expressed this view in response to a brief questionnaire distributed by UNISON. It was shown that secretaries generally believe their skills are undervalued and their abilities and experience ignored. They feel increasingly miscast since they no longer fulfil merely a support function, and seek recognition for the administrative nature of their tasks. Whilst moving into administrative posts for secretarial staff has always been difficult, a significant number have managed to break through the glass ceiling, subsequently demonstrating their administrative abilities. Recently, however, many secretaries feel the glass ceiling has been reinforced making such moves highly unlikely, if not impossible. This has come about in a number of ways.

Recruitment Strategies

University management believe current trends indicate that many future secretarial posts will be filled by graduates entering the job market for the first time. Academic managers may actually prefer to work with graduates who are, after all, the end products of their own occupational efforts. This challenges secretaries' future career prospects as well as their present position with regard to mobility between university posts. This contrasts with the Industrial Society Report (Allcock, 1993, p. 9) where only 2 per cent of managers in the private sector considered a degree necessary for secretarial/administrative posts.

Internal advertisements for administrative posts have often implied that the successful candidate will be a graduate. UNISON have requested that junior administrative posts are advertised in a way which positively invites secretarial staff to apply. To date this request has been ignored. Indeed, advertisements now explicitly seek 'recent or new graduates' and many secretaries who feel they are well qualified in terms of ability and experience are excluded by this arbitrary artificial qualification barrier. This dismisses and ignores a valuable resource within the secretarial workforce and takes no account of years of experience of working with university processes and procedures, together with an expanding range of skills. Growing numbers of new graduates entering a depressed employment market seeking altern-ative routes to careers within administration and management ensure that there is no shortage of applicants (Carter, 1996, p. 13).

Setting unnecessarily high qualification requirements which act nevertheless as an important filter in the selection process, does not constitute good employment practice, and indeed is contrary to good equal opportunities practice. Secretaries internalize the negative view of their contribution implicit in this requirement and may perceive themselves as lacking in worth and value. Such lack of adequate recognition can be destructive and, according to Taylor (1994), represents a power-ful form of oppression leading to marginalization, lack of confidence and motiva-tion. It can also lead to misunderstandings both by line managers and by secretaries themselves, about the requirements for career progression into administrative grades. Thus able secretarial staff fail to apply for senior posts as they arise simply because they feel they would not be considered. This negative attitude reinforces manage-ment view that the number of suitable candidates within the secretarial staff pool is low, and strengthens the desire to recruit graduates.

It is important to note, however, that an increasing number of existing secret-arial staff at Wessex University are graduates, usually gaining their qualification whilst in employment. Denied the opportunity at completion of compulsory educa-tion, a growing number of mature secretaries are currently enrolled on degree programmes. In one faculty 15 per cent of secretarial staff are graduates or students on degree courses, both undergraduate and postgraduate. These studies are under-taken in addition to full-time or part-time employment, and family responsibilities. There has been no attempt by university management to determine just how many of its current secretarial staff are graduates. Consequently, there is a lack of aware-ness about the quality of the skills repertoire of existing staff.

Yet, the status accorded to graduates who take up administrative posts is often higher than that of a secretary who has progressed into an administrative post. Most administrators have some form of secretarial support, whereas secretaries who become administrators are often expected to provide their own secretarial support. This puts them at a disadvantage in terms of their position within the social divi-sions existing in higher education administration. Secretaries are aware of the prob-lem of social stratification within the administrative hierarchy. Status remains a significant factor, and the importance accorded to different staff categories is influ-ential in shaping attitudes of those responsible for employment and promotion. At Wessex University several layers of managerial hierarchies operate: at committee and central administrative level, faculty level, and departmental level. This creates con-flicts and power struggles between academic and non-academic decision-makers, producing further stratification based upon class.

Elitist attitudes towards occupations in higher education are compounded by gender divisions which play an important role in maintaining the low status of secretarial staff. Nationally, men make up around a quarter of clerical staff, of all genres (Equal Opportunities Commission, 1995). Within 'old universities' the number of men in clerical work is fewer at only 11 per cent. However, when the number of men in the top grade 6 post is considered in relation to their representation in the clerical population, this increases significantly to over 27 per cent (Universities and Colleges Employers Association, 1994, p. 4.4). At Wessex University the number of men in clerical posts is small. Despite this, the proportion of men in grade 6 posts (21.4 per cent) is significantly higher than the proportion of women in the same grade in relation to their general distribution (Equal Opportunities Monitoring Report, 1995). This makes the lack of career progression opportunities for female secretaries even more significant.

The outcome of these developments is to reinforce existing impediments to career progression for secretarial staff within higher education. In Wessex University in particular, these barriers now have two important aspects. First, the growing number of graduates who are available for recruitment into secretarial posts and who may expect more encouragement from managers whose own academic experience accords greater value to academic qualifications. Second, the increasing number of men who undertake secretarial work, whose status within a gendered, devalued occupation, is even now different to that of female secretaries, poses a serious threat. The hierarchical nature of male dominated organizations such as higher education establishments, coupled with the academic ethos, may encourage recruitment strategies which amount to 'like employing like' This has serious implications for female secretarial staff unless their status is acknowledged and the value placed upon their contribution is adequately recognized.

Conclusion

It has been argued that both general and specific factors account for the changes which have occurred in the secretarial role. Positive response to these changes, both in terms of academic interest and action by employers, has been patchy. Whilst senior management may be sincere in the belief that equal opportunities statements and policies will bring about real changes in real lives, this may represent a blinkered view of the world, based upon male experiences at the top of the male hierarchy. The experiences for women, and members of other disadvantaged groups continue to be very different (Forbes, 1996). Where a firm commitment at the highest level to removing obstacles which prevent career advances is lacking, meaningful change will be limited.

Clearly Wessex University has made progress towards implementing measures to improve the future position of female employees and in provision of training facilities for secretarial staff. This is certainly a step in the right direction. University managers acknowledge a problem exists, although they fail to recognize the full magnitude of the problem and the need for a considerable level of cultural change within the organization. Change affecting a limited number of individuals will do little alone. A firm commitment to more radical approaches to improve the situation for large numbers of secretaries is required. Intentions expressed in connection with Opportunity 2000 need to be translated into positive action.

A pressing need exists for attitudinal change in respect of the value placed upon the work women do. This applies to higher education administration and teaching, employment generally, and the multiplicity of roles women adopt in respect of their paid employment and family responsibilities. Discarding stereotypical assumptions about secretaries is crucial to developing a more realistic image of the role. Without positive changes in basic perspectives of women's identities by employers, society generally, and by women themselves, little progress towards equal opportunities and, hence, career advancement will be achievable (Spencer and Taylor, 1994, p. 32).

References

ALLCOCK, D. (1993) *Typecast: Unlocking Secretaries' Potential*, London: The Industrial Society.

BRAVERMAN, H. (1974) *Labour and Monopoly Capital: The Degradation of Work in the Twentieth Century*, New York: Monthly Review Press.

BUSINESS IN THE COMMUNITY (1992) 'Opportunity 2000: Towards a Balanced Workforce', *Local Government Management*.

CARTER, M. (1996) 'Going against type', *The Independent*, 12 December.

CLEMENT, B. (1996) 'Tide of change in typing pool', *Independent*, 29 August 1996.

COCKBURN, C. (1991) *In the Way of Women: Men's Resistance to Sex Equality in Organisations*, London: Macmillan.

COYLE, A. (1995) *Women and Organisational Change*: Equal Opportunities Commission.

CROMPTON, R. (1994) 'Occupational trends and women's employment patterns', in LINDLEY, R. (ed.) *Labour Market Structures and Prospects for Women*: Equal Opportunities Commission.

CROMPTON, R. and JONES, G. (1984) *White-collar Proletariat: Deskilling and Gender in Clerical Work*, London: Macmillan.

DOWNING, H. (1980) 'Word processors and the oppression of women', in FORESTER, T. (ed.) *The Microelectronics Revolution*, Oxford: Basil Blackwell.

EQUAL OPPORTUNITIES COMMISSION (1995) *Equal Opportunities Review*, **54.**

FEARFULL, A. (1996) 'Clerical workers, clerical skills: Case studies from credit management', *New Technology, Work and Employment*, **11**, 1, pp. 55–65.

FORBES, I. (1996) 'The privatisation of sex equality policy', in LOVENDUSKI, J. and NORRIS, P. (eds) *Parliamentary Affairs*, **49**, 1, pp. 143–60.

GALLIE, D. and WHITE, M. (1993) *Employee Commitment and the Skills Revolution*, London: Policy Studies Institute.

GAME, A. and PRINGLE, R. (1984) *Gender at Work*, London: Pluto Press.

HAKIM, C. (1978) 'Sexual division within the labour force: Occupational segregation', *Department of Employment Gazette*, November.

HEPBURN, J. (1991) *Secretaries: Still a Wasted Asset?* London: The Industrial Society.

KANTER, R.M. (1977) *Men and Women of the Corporation*, New York: Basic Books.

LOCKWOOD, D. (1989) *The Blackcoated Worker: A Study in Class Consciousness*, 2nd ed. (Postscript), Oxford: Clarendon.

LOVENDUSKI, J. and RANDALL, V. (1993) *Contemporary Feminist Politics: Women and Power in Britain*, Oxford: Oxford University Press.

LOWE, G.S. (1987) *Women in the Administrative Revolution: The Feminization of Clerical Work*, Cambridge: Polity Press.

MAIR, M. and POVALL, M. (1995) 'Secretaries . . . onwards and upwards? The future role of the secretary', Joint Secretarial Development Network and Industrial Society Report.

PHILLIPS, A. and TAYLOR, B. (1980) 'Sex and skill: Notes towards a feminist economics', *Feminist Review*, 6, pp. 79–88.

POVALL, M., COLE, P., ELKIN, G., GEORGE, S., LONG, V. and MARSHALL, V. (1991) 'The secretary releasing the real potential', Secretarial Development Network, Project Report.

PRINGLE, R. (1992) 'What is a secretary?', in McDOWELL, L. and PRINGLE, R. *Defining Women*, Cambridge: Polity Press.

PRINGLE, R. (1993) 'Male secretaries', in WILLIAMS, C. (ed.) *Doing Women's Work: Men in Nontraditional Occupations*, London: Sage Publications.

REED PERSONNEL (1996) *The Changing Secretarial Role*, Survey Report.

SPENCER, L. and TAYLOR, M. (1994) *Participation and Progress in the Labour Market: Key Issues for Women*, Department for Employment Research Series No 35.

TATE APPOINTMENTS (1995) *Secretaries Could Become a Thing of the Past*, Survey on changing roles.

TAYLOR, C. (1994) 'The politics of recognition', in GUTMANN, A. (ed.) *Multiculturalism: Examining the Politics of Recognition*, Princeton, NJ: Princeton University Press.

UNIVERSITIES AND COLLEGES EMPLOYERS ASSOCIATION (1995) *University and College Statistics — 1994.*

WALBY, S. (1990) *Theorizing Patriarchy*, Oxford: Basil Blackwell.

WESSEX UNIVERSITY (1995) *Equal Opportunities Monitoring Report.*

8 Incorporation or Alienation? Resisting the Gendered Discourses of Academic Appraisal

Robyn Thomas

Introduction

It has been well established in the literature that universities are patriarchal institutions where male hegemony is seen as natural and unproblematic (Blackstone and Fulton, 1975; Spender, 1982; Simeone, 1987; Stiver-Lie and O'Leary, 1990; Acker, 1992; Heward and Taylor, 1992; Bagilhole, 1993; Davies et al., 1994; Morley, 1994; Morley and Walsh, 1995, 1996). Universities, as with other organizations, may be perceived as gendered cultures, made up of a network of interwoven discourses, which permeate the entire organization and which work to subordinate women. The notion of a gendered university culture covers all the taken-for-granted, unquestioned attitudes, behaviour, values and basic assumptions about the nature and role of the institution and the role of women within it. It includes the wealth of practices which render women academics' participation undervalued, unrecognized and marginalized, leading to an overwhelming feeling of 'otherness' (Acker, 1980). University cultures can therefore be seen to present a set of problems for women in terms of forming their identity as academics. They are confronted with a whole range of discourses which shape their notions of femininity but at the same time face organizational rules and practices which are male dominated (Mills, 1993). The recent changes in the management of universities and the academic profession present new challenges and opportunities for women academics. The research presented in this chapter questions to what extent, and in what ways, the new discourses of higher education management have intensified the problems facing women academics.[1]

Discourses of New Public Management

The last 15 years has witnessed a period of cultural change in universities which have challenged the traditional role and image of higher education and the academic profession.

A key feature of this so-called transformation has been the introduction of techniques designed to monitor performance rendering individual academics and academic cost centres more accountable for their performance. This has resulted in the introduction of performance indicators and standardized output measures to monitor performance. As part of this package of change, academic appraisal forms one element in a disciplinary matrix, regulating and normalizing the academic, bringing work in line with the prevailing government ethos on managing public service professionals.

Traditional discourse on appraisal gives an image of rationality, technicism and neutrality. Despite research showing the problems of bias and subjectivity in appraisal (Dipboye, 1985; Williams and Walker, 1985; De Meuse, 1987; Hedge and Kavanagh, 1988; Sackett et al., 1991), it is often argued that appraisal can serve to promote equal opportunities (EO) through the unbiased judging of performance according to formalized, objective performance criteria and the provision of systematic feedback on professional development and career planning (Hansard Society Commission, 1990). The literature on 'effective' appraisal tends to focus on the appraisal instrument, debating whether it should emphasize development or assessment, whilst ignoring the wider organizational, social and political context in which it operates. Recent interest in appraisal, however, has shifted attention from its role in managing performance to that of the management of meaning and the social construction of identity through appraisal (Smircich and Morgan, 1982; Townley, 1992; Bowles and Coates, 1993; Grint, 1993). Drawing on the Foucauldian concepts of discourse, it is suggested that appraisal can be seen, not as a mirror, reflecting the activity of the organization, but as a gaze which renders the academic visible (but only those activities which are valued in the new culture), to both the organization and the individual themselves (Townley, 1992). Appraisal works as a normalizing mechanism, through which the individual is judged, compared and ranked against a standard (gendered) norm. It tells the individual academic the extent to which he or she meets the norms of performance and how this performance ranks in comparison with others. Appraisal can be understood as an 'information panopticon' (Zuboff, 1988), the panopticon being an architectural design (originally for prisons) with a central observation tower around which prisoners may be housed, enabling effective surveillance. It therefore enables the appraiser to 'see everything', to monitor all aspects of the individual's work making it possible for 'a single gaze to see everything constantly' (Foucault, 1977, p. 173). Here appraisal operates to *create* an individual's self-identity. It does this through a form of confessional whereby individuals are constantly placed in situations where they are forced to think about themselves and simultaneously provide the answers (Coates, 1994). In this way, appraisal operates as the 'perfect disciplinary practice' (Foucault, 1977, p. 193) judging the extent to which the new cultural values have been internalized and thus brings about the effects of which it seeks knowledge.

This research seeks to examine how women academics' self identities are shaped by the gendered culture of the institution and the functioning of academic appraisal. It examines women academics' responses to the new discourses of higher education management; whether women have internalized the new norms of performance, or whether they have been able to resist the normalizing discourses. The research examines how the new discourses have affected women academics' experiences of academic work and their identities. Focusing on the subjectivizing and normalizing aspects of appraisal, therefore, the research questions the extent to which women have been able to intervene in the shaping of the 'new academic' and have their voices heard in the gendered academy.

Background to the Cases

The research is based on two case study universities, one 'old' and one 'new', named Univille and Polytown respectively. Thirty-four women were interviewed (19 in Univille and 15 in Polytown), from across the hierarchy, using a semi-structured interview technique. In addition, interviews were carried out with the personnel director of each institution, to gain background information. In common with other UK universities, both institutions had few women from minority groups in all categories of staff, particularly academic staff. The women interviewed in this study were all white and able bodied, and, except in one case, heterosexual.

Univille is a well established university. It was originally set up as an institution of technology and this is still reflected today in the high profile of science and technology within the institution. It is ranked amongst the top 15 universities for its research, with many of the Schools gaining a grade 5 in the last Research Assessment Exercise. Not surprisingly, given its technological roots, the gender profile of the academic staff is considerably worse than the national average. Women make up 10 per cent (38) of the total academic staff, with 4 per cent (2) of professors being female, 7 per cent (9) of readers and senior lecturers and 15 per cent (27) of lecturers. The university has only recently published an EO policy and an EO committee is planned for the future. No formal monitoring is carried out, except for annual returns to the Higher Education Statistics Agency. Appraisal has been running for six years, with all interviews being undertaken by the head of department. A standard university-wide appraisal instrument is used, which includes a section recording a range of quantitative performance indicators, measuring student feedback, publications and research funding.

Polytown was originally established as a polytechnic in 1970 and, along with other polytechnics, was granted university status in 1992. Like many former polytechnics it has developed strengths in teaching and, whilst having a good reputation for its consultancy, research has not been of primary importance. The gender profile of the institution is considerably better than both Univille and the national average. Women make up 33 per cent (183) of academic staff, with 19 per cent (6) of HOD/ Dean grade being women, 19 per cent (23) of principal lecturers and 38 per cent (154) of lecturers/senior lecturers. The formalized system of equal opportunities is well developed, with the institution having both an EO policy and committee as well as carrying out monitoring of staff across the hierarchy and of appointments and promotions. An equal opportunities audit has recently been carried out, confirming the gender imbalance of staff, particularly at senior levels. Appraisal has been running for three years. The form and implementation of appraisal tends to be rather *ad hoc*, differing between departments, ranging from ratings based through to self assessment. Appraisal is carried out by the head of department and principal lecturers, with appraisees' choosing their preferred appraiser. This variety of forms of appraisal reflects the decentralized structure of the institution, where individual departments act fairly autonomously in their day-to-day management.

Discourses of Subordination

The respondents, in both institutions highlighted the various day-to-day difficulties associated with being a woman academic in a male dominated organization.

The culture in Univille was typified as being traditional and paternalistic, made up of 'good chaps' in the 'gentleman's club' (Maddock and Parkin, 1993). As one woman observed:

> It is difficult to be taken seriously in the University hierarchy. . . . A lot of men here are fine about women members of staff as long as they keep in their place.

Superimposed on to this, in recent years, has been a move towards a more competitive culture, based on a managerialist model of 'go-getting, insurgent, ruthless and tough' management (Newman, 1995, p. 17). Whilst this was more pronounced in some departments than others (particularly those with grade 5 research ratings), there was a general feeling expressed by the women in the case study that the culture had, in recent years, become more competitive, individualistic and focused on quantifiable outputs, mainly publications: 'It seems to be about counting and it is in fact playing the numbers game of how many papers you've written, how much money you've raised'.

Within Polytown, however, there was a general acknowledgment that, superficially, issues of equal opportunities were espoused. However this was seen to be mainly 'lip service', or a 'political gesture' and very little was done to address the underlying structures of inequality, which were considered to be 'shocking' and 'embedded in discrimination'. As one woman observed: 'My gut feeling is that it is a bit of a sham. There are a lot of wordy statements coming out and the Institution puts itself forward as being equal opportunities. I think, at the end of the day, it is a bit of a con'.

However, there were considerable departmental variations. Some of the women interviewed worked in departments comprising of a significant number of female colleagues. Here, there were comments that the day-to-day working atmosphere was more 'comfortable', despite the institution as a whole being patriarchal. These departments were in subject areas (notably education and social work), where the women had chosen to move into higher education primarily to teach. Thus the competitive practices of publication rates and income generation were less obvious parts of their day-to-day lives. However, as in the case of Univille, the women commented on the general intensification of work in recent years, brought about by increased student numbers and a marked shift towards valuing quantifiable research output and income generating consultancy over course administration and teaching.

In both universities, the women respondents commented that the recent changes in the management of higher education had a marked effect on the nature of academic work and professional identity. There was a general consensus of opinion that working conditions had worsened and that the job was less pleasurable, with longer hours, greater stress, greater pressures to perform, increased monitoring and accountability all being cited by the interviewees: 'It's turning more instrumental, more and more competitive. There's less room for creativity, more pressure to conform in your activities and in your research model'.

The women in both institutions noted the changing norms of performance with the increased pressures to publish and produce quantifiable research output. The generation of research publications was increasingly seen as the most valued activity by senior management. Clearly research has always been of great importance in Univille but in recent years there has been the shift towards counting research output and generating research grants in a new 'macho culture' (Maddock and Parkin, 1993) of performance.

Constituting the New Academic

The functioning of appraisal was perceived very differently in the two cases. In Univille, appraisal was seen to be operating very much as a symbol of the 'new order', driving the changes within the institution towards a more performance oriented culture. Here, the 'normalizing gaze' of appraisal was seen to be producing a narrower and specific model of academic work. This was a model which many of the women were either unwilling through choice, or unable through material circumstances, to engage in. As one woman commented: 'Unless you conform to the norm you are excluded — it's a culture of accumulated petty exclusion. You have to conform to this narrow norm', and, similarly: '. . . It is yet another means of trying to mould everyone to a particular norm. It is telling you which hoops you have to jump through, and what you have to do in order to conform.'

However, superficially, the operation of appraisal seems to differ in Polytown. In several departments, appraisal was seen to be a 'non-event', a bureaucratic form filling exercise, where at best you managed to discuss timetabling issues. However, such responses may miss the more subtle workings of appraisal as a disciplinary technology and its role in the management of meaning: 'It is a little bit unreal, really. It would be much better if someone was controlling and watching and helping you develop throughout the year and then the year end process, at the end, would be better'. This is precisely its role. Through a once-a-year, often seemingly innocuous exercise, therefore, appraisal provides a continuous surveillance of performance in the form of monitoring of publications, amount of research funding gained, student feedback on teaching, and administrative functions carried out by the academic. For several respondents in Polytown, however, there were underlying messages about the new ethos of performance in the institution:

> I like appraisal as I like receiving feedback. It gives me a chance to discuss things with the head of department alone and to have an extensive conversation with him. . . . I felt like I got a telling off for not doing the research though. The subject of my research was brought up and what I was going to do about it. I told him I'd do the work during the summer — I've set a deadline.

In other departments the 'normalizing gaze' was much more explicit:

> Thinking about it now I realize that I'm really annoyed, I'm really angry. It is down right undermining because apart from not being valued for the work you do, you are constantly being told where you are not fulfilling what the head of department wants. You can't discuss what you are having difficulties with, you can't bring up anything negative.

Resisting the Gendered Gaze

In both cases there were women who, in a variety of ways, were attempting to resist the new discourses of management. For these women, resistance was at the forefront of their day-to-day activities within the gendered institutional culture. This was particularly the case for those women who had devoted their energies to teaching and student issues. The increased student numbers, and the perceived erosion in teaching standards — 'putting as many students as possible through the sausage machine', as one woman put it — was seen to be a further attack on their identity as members of the academic profession. Many women interviewees were questioning the new discourses of competition, asserting their values of academic service. This meant valuing student support work, having time for critical reflection, and developing teaching. However, the strategy of 'opting out' of the instrumental competition meant accepting that this would lead to further marginalization and the psychologically negative consequences on their self confidence and self worth of watching other academics' careers advance. However, in the new higher education environment, those who perform to the new norms are favoured with lower timetables, better salaries, promotion and status. Women who do not perform become 'ghettoized' as an academic 'underclass'. A frequent comment made by the women was that their career aims were to 'enjoy my work', which in effect meant 'opting out' of the career ladder, as illustrated by the following quote:

> No I don't have any particular ambitions in terms of moving up the hierarchy. I think my ambition would be to feel comfortable in my job, doing good things for my students and to gain joy from that. But I don't particularly want to progress. What I enjoy about this job is being able to teach well.

However, the extent to which women could choose to 'opt out' differed in the two cases and between individuals. In Univille, the pressure to publish and keep research output up meant that developing an alternative career plan was becoming increasingly difficult due to the pressures generated in appraisal to reconceptualize yourself as the output oriented academic. Whereas in the past it was agreed that research was always the most valued aspect of the academic role, at least in the old university sector, this had been in a far less competitive, output orientated, macho manner. In addition, those individuals who concentrated on other aspects of the job had still been accepted within the culture. This had now changed and the pressures to conform to the new norms of performance were very evident:

> ... I get told to stop concentrating on my teaching and the other things I do, and to concentrate on writing some straightforward, heavyweight articles. Then I will be all right and will be promoted. It is always that, telling me to stop doing the things that I do and concentrate on other things that are deemed more important. I could do what they say but I don't because I don't want to. It's a matter of principle really.

> ... Look for God's sake, come clean, you are either supportive or you are not but don't give me this kind of soft soap. I have said to myself, 'sod all of that'. I have decided to stop getting screwed up about all of these things. If that means not being quite so effective and not being so nice to my colleagues, stopping letting them treat me as Mum ... then tough. ...

In Polytown, there was, however, still accommodation made for those devoting their energies to teaching, however, this had never been seen as a route to promotion:

> I have never had the view that I want career progression. I have always taken the view that I want to enjoy the job and get the most out of it in terms of what interests me regardless of promotion. The nice thing about my job is that you can direct it towards what you are doing.

> I prefer just to get on with the teaching — it is not without its problems but its easier than getting involved with the politics of management. I have a policy of doing what I want to do because I find it interesting.

The strategy of 'opting out' results in further isolation for women academics and perpetuates male dominance within the culture. What is more, it sustains women academics' silence in the decision making process. As Morley (1994) comments: 'Women are then caught in a paradoxical situation in which resistance reproduces discrimination' (1994, p. 198).

There were women who were choosing to 'opt in' to the new cultural norms. Under appraisal, it was felt that the normalizing gaze was made more visible and it was clearer to see what the 'perfect professional' was meant to do. Thus appraisal was the ideal mechanism for women to 'shout about their achievements', as one woman put it. Appraisal offered the opportunity to highlight work that had been done, to 'set the record straight': 'It is an opportunity to present what you're doing in some systematic way, and inform, so that it debugs rumour and provides the opportunity to put the record straight'. Women who were active researchers, had long publications lists, with highly productive research profiles, found it easiest to comply with the new competitive climate. In the gendered reward system of new higher education, those without domestic commitments find it easier to 'play like men' (Morley, 1994). Corresponding with the findings of other research examining the changing cultures of public sector organizations (Maddock and Parkin, 1993) those who were able to work an 80 hour week and produce the research output were managing to compete in the new culture. However, this 'gender-blind culture' assumes that you have no domestic commitments. Furthermore, it ignores the time taken on emotional labour that women academics frequently undertake in the department. As one woman commented: 'There may be good reasons why someone doesn't achieve their objectives. Those who do well in this department . . . their personal life is under a lot of pressure — there's no getting away from that — they look like they're on cocaine!' Under the new discourses of management, the academic process is increasingly commodified (Willmott, 1995). The new disciplinary technologies are seen to promote a 'virility culture' (Walsh, 1994), reinforcing and reasserting the dominant masculine discourses of the university organization. The questioning should not be, therefore, why women fail to compete in the 'academic game' (McAuley, 1987) but of the so-called naturalness of masculine norms upon which the university is constructed.

Conclusion

To what extent have the women in the two cases challenged the ways in which they are defined, labelled and classified as subordinate members of the institution? Resistance, for women, comes through taking advantage of the 'tactical polyvalence' (Sawicki, 1994) of discursive practices. It is achieved through challenging the discourses of masculine dominance within the institution. As Foucault argues:

> Discourse transmits and produces power; it reinforces it, but also undermines and exposes it, renders it fragile and makes it possible to thwart it. (Foucault, 1984, p. 101)

Some of the women interviewed could be seen as more accepting of the prevailing norms of performance. Appraisal provided them with the opportunity to 'claim their rightful place' as efficient, productive academics, by co-opting into the masculinist culture. Thus in both case studies, appraisal offered the women to think more strategically about their careers by making it clear what the new norms of performance were — telling the women which 'hoops you have to jump through'. Under the 'moral technology' of management (Foucault, 1977), the new academic is reconstituted as a standardized, rationalized, efficient, genderless worker. Those who 'rise to the challenge' and embrace the new values and norms may do well in this new macho culture. Under a liberal/equal opportunities framework, appraisal can be seen to provide career advice and mentorship, breaking down the barriers to advancement within universities. However, this does no more than enable women to become surrogate men (Crompton and Le Feuvre, 1992). Those academics with domestic commitments, or who have invested their energies in teaching and administration find it difficult to be incorporated into this new ethos — and these are more likely to be women.

Appraisal can be seen to function as a catalyst for changing, creating and reinforcing the new culture. This has presented new challenges and opportunities for women academics. Within Univille, the strength of the 'panoptic gaze' was felt by the women academics, where appraisal was seen to emphasize the managerialist thrust coming from central government imbued with masculine values of competitive management. Those who did not conform to the new norms of performance were finding it increasingly difficult to fit in. In Polytown, however, whilst the women also commented on the moves towards a more intensive, competitive culture, there was not such a narrow academic norm. Thus, it was felt that a range of career profiles were at least accommodated, if not rewarded.

In both cases, appraisal can be seen as failing the women academics in the masculinist culture of the university. This research suggests that there is a need to reconceptualize academic careers to accept different career strategies. Appraisal can be used to create a culture more receptive to women academics' needs and experiences, emphasizing a more balanced profile of the academic job. This holds the potential to allow individuals, both women and men, to concentrate on different aspects of the job and to recognize the important role played by those individuals who devote their energies to teaching and pastoral duties. Many women respondents carried out essential work within the department but this was neither valued nor rewarded. What is more, with the recent changes in the management of higher education, the academic role may be seen as being more narrowly defined, less accommodating of difference, and a more gendered model of 'macho management'. The implications from these two case studies suggests that women academics may have to face stark choices. The women in both cases face a constant struggle of having to prove themselves as legitimate members of the organization and not accept the disabling discourses and thereby 'internalise the oppression' (Morley, 1994). Some women have chosen to 'opt in' and embrace the new discourses of competition. Alternatively, many women have chosen, or been forced through material circumstances, to 'opt out', resisting the normalizing discourses. However, as Ferguson (1984) observes, when it comes to resisting the dominant discourses, 'one can resist and survive, but one seldom both resists and prospers' (1984, p. 191). In these two cases resistance may result in a denial of material rewards and career progression, a loss of self esteem as a member of the academic profession and the perpetuation of women's silence at senior policy making level.

Note

1   In presenting this research, it is necessary to explain my 'state of being' (Coleman, 1991). Being a female academic engaged in research on female academics, it would be impossible (as well as misguided) to attempt to approach the research from a disinterested and objective stance. As with the women interviewed in this research, I too am partly constituted by the discourses of higher education management and the making of knowledge and reflecting on my theorizing, further contributes to this process. However, I am aware that I have also, to a certain extent, 'shut out' much of what has been said or written; not to do so would result in despair, working in a male dominated academic field and institution, located in a strongly patriarchal Welsh Valleys community. As Acker (1994), comments: 'The gendering of academic practice is a difficult terrain for women academics to write about . . . because of the danger of being thought to be "obsessed" or showing pique and disappointment' (1994, p. 70). How true.

References

ACKER, S. (1980) 'Women, the other academics', *British Journal of Sociology of Education*, **1**, 1, pp. 81–91.

ACKER, S. (1992) 'New perspectives on an old problem: The position of women academics in British higher education', *Higher Education*, **24**, pp. 57–75.

ACKER, S. (1994) *Gendered Education: Sociological Reflections on Women, Teaching and Feminism*, Buckingham: Open University Press.

BAGILHOLE, B. (1993) 'Survivor in a male preserve: A study of British women academics' experiences and perceptions of discrimination in a UK university', *Higher Education*, **26**, pp. 431–47.

BLACKSTONE, T. and FULTON, O. (1975) 'Sex discrimination among university teachers: A British-American comparison', *British Journal of Sociology*, **6**, 3, pp. 261–76.

BOWLES, M.L. and COATES, G. (1993) 'Image and substance: The management of performance as rhetoric or reality?', *Personnel Review*, **22**, 2, pp. 3–21.

COATES, G. (1994) 'Performance appraisal as icon: Oscar-winning performance or dressing to impress?', *The International Journal of Human Resource Management*, **5**, 1, pp. 167–91.

COLEMAN, G. (1991) *Investigating Organisations: A Feminist Approach*, Occasional Paper 37, Bristol: SAUS.

CROMPTON, R. and LE FEUVRE, N. (1992) 'Gender and bureaucracy: Women in finance in Britain and France', in SAVAGE, M. and WITZ, A. (eds) *Gender and Bureaucracy*, Oxford: Basil Blackwell.

DAVIES, S., LUBELSKA, C. and QUINN, J. (eds) (1994) *Changing the Subject: Women in Higher Education*, London: Taylor and Francis.

DE MEUSE, K.P. (1987) 'A review of the effects of non-verbal cues on the performance appraisal process', *Journal of Occupational Psychology*, **60**, pp. 207–26.

DIPBOYE, R.L. (1985) 'Some neglected variables in research on discrimination in appraisal', *Academy of Management Review*, **10**, 1, pp. 116–27.

FERGUSON, K. (1984) *The Feminist Case Against Bureaucracy*, Philadelphia: Temple University Press.

FOUCAULT, M. (1977) *Discipline and Punish: the Birth of the Prison*, London: Allen Lane.

FOUCAULT, M. (1984) 'Polemics, politics and problematizations: An interview', in RABINOW, P. (ed.) *The Foucault Reader*, London: Penguin.

GRINT, K. (1993) 'What's wrong with performance appraisals: A critique and a suggestion', *Human Resource Management Journal*, **3**, 3, pp. 61–77.

HANSARD SOCIETY COMMISSION (1990) *The Report of the Hansard Society Commission on Women at the Top*, London: Hansard Society for Parliamentary Government.

HEDGE, J.W. and KAVANAGH, M.J. (1988) 'Improving the accuracy of performance evaluation: Comparison of the three methods of training', *Journal of Applied Psychology*, **73**, 1, pp. 68–73.

HEWARD, C. and TAYLOR, P. (1992) 'Women at the top in higher education: Equal opportunities policies in action?', *Policy and Politics*, **20**, 2, pp. 111–21.

MADDOCK, S. and PARKIN, D. (1993) 'Gender cultures: Women's choices and strategies at work', *Women in Management Review*, **8**, 2, pp. 3–9.

MCAULEY, J. (1987) 'Women academics: A case study', in SPENCER, A. and PODMORE, D. (eds) *In a Man's World: Essays on Women in Male Dominated Professions*, London: Tavistock, pp. 158–81.

MILLS, A.J. (1993) 'Organizational discourse and the gendering of identity', in HASSARD, J. and PARKER, M. (eds) *Postmodernism and Organizations*, London: Sage.

MORLEY, L. (1994) 'Glass ceiling or iron cage: Women in UK academia', *Gender, Work and Organization*, **1**, 4, pp. 194–204.

MORLEY, L. and WALSH, V. (1995) *Feminist Academics: Creative Agents for Change*, London: Taylor and Francis.

MORLEY, L. and WALSH, V. (1996) *Breaking Boundaries: Women in Higher Education*, London: Taylor and Francis.

NEWMAN, J. (1995) 'Gender and cultural change', in ITZIN, C. and NEWMAN, J. (eds) *Gender, Culture and Organizational Change*, London: Routledge.

SACKETT, P.R., DUBOIS, G.L.Z. and NOE, A.W. (1991) 'Tokenism in performance evaluation: The effects of work group representation on male, female, and white–black differences in performance ratings', *Journal of Applied Psychology*, **76**, 2, pp. 262–7.

SAWICKI, J. (1994) 'Foucault, feminism, and questions of identity', in GUTTING, G. (ed.) *The Cambridge Companion to Foucault*, Cambridge: Cambridge University Press.

SIMEONE, A. (1987) *Academic Women: Working towards Equality*, MA: Bergin and Harvey.

SMIRCICH, L. and MORGAN, G. (1982) 'Leadership: The management of meaning', *Journal of Applied Behavioural Science*, **18**, 3, pp. 257–73.

SPENDER, D. (1982) 'Sex bias', in WARREN-PIPER, D. (ed.) *Is Higher Education Fair?*, SRHE.

STIVER-LIE, S. and O'LEARY, (eds) (1990) *Storming the Tower: Women in the Academic World*, London: Kogan Page.

TOWNLEY, B. (1990) 'The politics of performance appraisal: Lessons on the introduction of appraisal into UK universities', *Human Resource Management*, **1**, pp. 27–44.

TOWNLEY, B. (1992) 'In the eye of the gaze: The constitutive role of performance appraisal', in BARRAR, P. and COOPER, C.L. (eds) *Managing Organisations in 1992: Strategic Responses*, London: Routledge.

WALSH, V. (1994) 'Virility culture: Academia and managerialism in higher education', in EVANS, M., GOSLING, J. and SELLER, A. (eds) *Agenda for Gender, Discussion Papers on Gender and the Organisation of Higher Education*, University of Kent at Canterbury.

WILLIAMS, R.S. and WALKER, J. (1985) 'Sex differences in performance ratings: A research note', *Journal of Occupational Psychology*, **58**, pp. 331–7.

WILLMOTT, H. (1995) 'Managing the academics: Commodification and control in the development of university education in the UK', *Human Relations*, **48**, 9, pp. 1–35.

ZUBOFF, S. (1988) *In the Age of the Smart Machine: The Future of Work and Power*, London: Heinemann.

Collective Action: Standing Still or Moving Forward?

9 Creating Space: The Development of a Feminist Research Group

Avril Butler

Introduction

This chapter is an outcome of my initiative to create a space in the academy where feminist voices could be heard and strengthened. In it I describe the processes involved in the recent development of a feminist research group at the university where I teach. I am a full-time senior lecturer in social work in an English university where, after 10 years in temporary and short-term contracts, I occupy a permanent post. This experience of having been in a marginal position for a long period has made me very conscious of the power and privilege I now have as a permanent member of staff. I have tried to maintain this 'outsider-within' consciousness (Collins, 1991) and to challenge the hierarchical and elitist norms of higher education and am helped by my continuing marginal position as an out lesbian and feminist. In writing about the process of setting up the feminist research group I make no claim to speak for all members of the group. It is inevitably my own perspective. However, the process of writing has included a discussion in the group and circulation of the drafts for critical comment.

Creating Space

In different areas of my life I have experienced the 'discomfort and blockage' described by women of Libreria delle Donne di Milano as a deadening of my ability to think and to work as I would wish. They attribute this to the difficulty of being a woman in social relationships where 'those who are given pride of place have a man's body' (Libreria delle Donne di Milano, 1991, p. 114). In response to this I have actively sought out what I perceive as supportive networks which would help me to develop my own potential. There is significant literature about the importance of women's support to each other (Raymond, 1986; Ernst and Goodison, 1993; Steinem, 1992) and international accounts of the impact on individuals involved. For example Consuelo Rivera Fuentes describes the transformational effect of lesbians coming together in Chile (Fuentes, 1996). Liane Davis introduces her book about feminist social work in America by emphasizing the way in which it seems to be possible for women to create an alternative reality; one which allows self-validation and the emergence of alternative discourses (Davis, 1994). In identifying these support networks for myself, I find myself looking for particular features. Naomi Gottlieb et al. describe the distinctive attributes of feminist groups as including the absence of men in the group, an emphasis on social and political factors in women's lives, the development of women's own group facilitation skills and a decrease in women's isolation from each other (Gottlieb et al., 1983). This culture of sharing and an open acknowledgment of the political context for women working at the university was absent from most of my working experience.

In my work at a 'new' university I was feeling increasing pressure to produce research 'deliverables' and I felt isolated in my work. At the same time I felt intimidated by what I perceived to be a male-dominated and exclusive culture attached to research in the organization. Fortunately I recognized these feelings as consistent with those of other women in higher education not some personal inadequacy. As Louise Morley and Val Walsh point out:

> Feminist academics are required to perform and produce, with authority and excellence, in an organisational and social context which disempowers materially and psychologically. (Morley and Walsh, 1995, p. 2)

Louise Morley's work on the micro-politics of exclusion (Morley, 1994, 1995) offers a detailed analysis of the way in which these feelings are generated. Earlier, in 1993, inspired partly by Caroline Ramazanoglu's analysis of her experience of academia (Ramazanoglu, 1987), I had done some joint research into sexual harassment of women academics and its connections to other forms of offensive behaviour from male colleagues. We found that 85 per cent of the women who responded experienced offensive and undermining behaviour as part of their work (Butler and Landells, 1994). Having established that I was not suffering from some personal inadequacy but that the organizational culture I was working in was a hostile environment, one which reduced my ability to produce the work expected of me, I decided to seek institutional help to improve things. In its mission statement the university states that it places a high value on human resources and I therefore took it at its word and tried to engage my employer's support to improve my ability to meet performance targets. I had in mind a forum for sharing work experiences and ideas in an environment where the 'cut and thrust' of normal debate was replaced with attentive listening and constructive criticism.

In my annual staff appraisal interview I complained of a sense of isolation in my work and a need of supportive contact with other women. I was offered access to staff development funds which could be used to bring women together and explore the possibility of an ongoing forum. A colleague had previously made several attempts to establish a regular meeting for women in the department but it had not continued because of women's other commitments. As the idea had been welcomed, I decided to try again by offering a day-long meeting away from the university when we did not have the demands of teaching.

Dilemmas of Starting

Having set a date for an all-day workshop on the first day of the Easter vacation I encountered the first problem: Who was the group for and how should I advertise it? I had discussed the idea with friends who were 'on the margins'. By this I refer to those women who do not have a permanent or significant employment with the university. They include post-graduate students, hourly-paid lecturers, research assistants and women on temporary contracts; women who are not included in institutional directories, who may not receive standard correspondence and who are often excluded from staff meetings and staff development and training events. I was shocked to discover that the staff development budget was only intended for supporting full-time members of staff. This meant that financial support from the university was only available to those with the financial security of a full time salary whilst those on a small grant or paid only for their teaching or research were not eligible for it. This seemed to me to be an example of the hierarchical and exclusive nature of the culture and resolved to ensure that we did not simply accept the norm.

I was clear that I wanted the group to be open to all women who were experiencing a sense of isolation in their work, to be multi-disciplinary in nature and open to women of different status and relationships to the university. This breaking down of traditional hierarchical relationships was a key feature of the group and one which I knew might challenge some women's ability to participate. In an academic institution, where status and value tend to be attached to academic achievement and power, I anticipated that it would be important to create an environment in which all women felt able to share uncertainties and confusions as well as excitement and pride in our work and that for some women this would threaten their hard-won status and power in the organization. I will return to the issue of power and equality later. I also wanted to avoid the group being restricted to 'active researchers', women working on a project for the purpose of academic publication, as I consider that the distinction between work and research is a false one (Weiner 1995). The intention was to create a forum where the strengths of different perspectives and experiences could contribute to each other on equal terms. This openness to all, however, created some concerns for me that the group could be dominated by women who were already successfully part of the existing culture and who would bring that culture with them to the group. I also felt exposed by my audacity at inviting all these academics to an event which was both a part of and apart from the normal business of the university. I was worried that women would come with expectations that we could not meet; that we would be not academic enough; not stimulating enough, not feminist enough. . . .

I resolved the initial dilemma of who the group was for, by discussing it with other women who were interested. We agreed that the group was for women who were interested in feminist research. The decision to identify the group as feminist rather than simply for women has been a key feature in its identity. I believed that it was important that members shared a view that as women, we do not inhabit a fair and equal world and that, whilst we may be more or less privileged in different ways, we are also all oppressed because of our gender. I had no wish to define which feminist analyses or positions were valid and which were not, believing that leaving women to choose to call themselves feminists or not was more consistent with what we were trying to achieve. In the words of Barbara Du Bois:

> To address women's lives and experience in their own terms, to create theory grounded in the actual experience and language of women, is the central agenda for feminist social science and scholarship. (Du Bois, 1983, p. 108)

In advertising the group we used a 'snowball' approach. As we did not have the resources to send information to all women employed by, and connected with, the university, we produced an open invitation with a tear-off slip to circulate to women we thought might be interested, encouraging them to photocopy it and pass it on. This use of informal networks and information systems was intended to cross discipline boundaries and be as inclusive as possible. I am aware of the potential for this method to exclude those women not part of the established networks but felt it was better than some of the established information systems which privilege full-time employees over others.

The next dilemma in planning the day was concerned with power relationships in the group. How could we create a space which would encourage feminist process from the beginning? I was afraid that my own investment in the group would make it hard for me to let the group do its own work rather than work to my agenda. To avoid this a colleague offered to facilitate the first session of the day which was for negotiating the day's agenda and agreeing who would facilitate each session.

On the day the process worked very well, with different women facilitating and recording the decisions. One outcome was that we identified the aims of the group, which were to encourage collaborative working, to give members confidence in pursuing their interests and in develoing their work, and to give support in preparing work for publication. We decided that we wanted regular monthly meetings and periodic day-long meetings with themes. We would share/discuss work in progress and the group would be open to all women interested in feminist research/work. Since that first day we have had regular monthly two-hour meetings which have moved to different days of the week in order not to exclude individuals. We have learnt the importance of beginning each meeting with taking time for women to feel comfortable with each other and included as full members of the group, particularly as different women attend each time. Usually the first hour is spent in a combination of personal sharing of where we each are in terms of our work and what impinges on it and includes us talking about our feelings. In the second hour there is space for one woman to present an aspect of her work for discussion. Issues covered have included preparation for a PhD viva, discussion of the design and use of questionnaires, ethics in research with children, access to the internet, reports from conferences, a discussion of methodological issues and a critique of grounded theory, academic feminism and setting up a feminist research group. Attendance has been very variable ranging from 2 to 12 members.

Researching Ourselves

Because of my initial investment in the group, I have acted as secretary/coordinator. This meant holding a mailing list of women who had asked to be part of the group,

Table 9.1: Factors which were chosen by women in each group

What women found useful	Attended most	Attended less than 3
Initial day workshop	6	1
Time to talk and hear about individuals' work	6	2
Content and discussion of individuals' presentations	6	1
Feedback from conferences	5	1
Making contact with other feminists	5	4
Circulation of papers	3	2
Open seminar	2	—
Other	2	1

sending out notes, information about future meetings and papers for discussion. In summer 1995 I was concerned that the list may have included women who were no longer interested and sent a letter asking them to confirm their wish to stay on the list. Most women did this and, in January 1996, 28 women were on the mailing list although the attendance at the previous two meetings had been very low. In order to try to make sense of this and to find out what women valued about the group and what prevented their attending, I sent out a short questionnaire. This consisted of some pre-coded questions which are specified in Tables 9.1 and 9.2, and space for women to explain or elaborate on their answers.

I saw this research as acting as a vehicle of communication between this diverse and geographically widespread group of women who appeared to be un-likely ever to meet all together as a group, as the highest attendance had comprised less than half the women. I hoped that sending out the questionnaire, and the results in the form of this paper in its various drafts, would act as a means of developing the group, as well as answering my questions about why women came and why women chose to be on the mailing list and not come. Of the 15 women who responded, 10 had been part of the group from the beginning and included one principal lecturer, two full-time senior lecturers, one full-time lecturer, three post-graduate research students, one librarian, one associate lecturer and one hourly-paid lecturer. The remaining five had joined the group in the previous three months and included one principal lecturer, two post-graduate research students, one full-time senior lecturer and one student adviser (disabilities). The women were all over 30, six were under 40, six others between 40 and 50 and three over 50, which sug-gested that the group was not only of interest to women starting out on their career. Indeed, five of us had been in our current career for over 10 years, three others for over five, three for over three years and four were in their first two years. The group comprised one black woman and 14 white women and included both heterosexual women and lesbians. Nine of the 15 women had parental responsibilities and two of these were single parents.

I divided the responses between those who had attended less than three ses-sions (nine) and those who had been to several or most (six). The questions allowed women to tick as many factors as they wished. Discussion and sharing of work was seen as useful by all those who had a high attendance and two women with lower attendance. One woman in the former group said:

Table 9.2: Constraints on attendance at meetings

	Attended most	**Attended less than 3**
Pressure of other commitments	5	6
Timing of meetings clashing with other commitments	3	8
Having to travel to university specially	2	1
Reservations about the group	—	2
Other	1	—

> I get ideas about how to do my research from hearing about other women's. It's good to know I'm not the only one who gets confused or unsure. The group makes research feel exciting and gives me confidence in an area where I lack experience.

The two women with lower attendance made the following comments:

> Encouraging to see this sort of support for feminist academics going forward. I've been able to refer post-graduate students to this group — very important.

These women, although not able to attend much themselves, said they valued it and encouraged others to come.

Making contact with other feminists was the factor which was consistently high in both groups and women made the following comments:

> It has enabled me to have real contact with staff/students at the university. It has also given me support in my own studies — overcoming a sense of isolation.

> I am pleased to support other women involved in research and am grateful for their support and friendship.

It seems that for some women the very fact of being a member of the group is enough to make them feel part of something supportive.

Because of the high number of women on the mailing list and the low attendance I was particularly interested in what women said interfered with their attendance. Table 9.2 shows this result. In retrospect it may have been interesting to know whether the other commitments which women had were social and domestic or associated with work but I did not make this distinction in the questionnaire.

One woman said:

> As I'm not actually a feminist researcher, it is sometimes hard to justify taking the time from my job.

Two women made reference to reservations about the appropriateness of their membership:

> My current research is not specifically relevant to feminism although I consider myself a feminist. I felt unsure whether this made me a relevant group member.

As a student I feel slightly uncertain about whether it is wholly appropriate for me to attend.

This comment echoed with another about power relationships in the group:

I found it difficult because two members were either students on the course of which I was programme leader or my supervisee in relation to their dissertation. I didn't have the time to raise the issue of power or even the energy.

Exploring the Issues

This last quote illustrates the problems of an 'open group' in which we are seeking to establish a 'moral equality of those who seek education and those who teach' (Humm, 1991, p. 52). Discomfort can be created for both students and teachers, in part because of the fact that the former are assessed by the latter. Maggie Humm, in her article about Women's Studies, says that this fact of assessment produces 'an artificial relationship, initiated and continued for a particular purpose within a particular framework' (Humm, 1991, p. 52). I suggest that the particular framework for academic relationships is one which maintains inequality. It depends on hierarchical structures in which some people and their contributions are seen as more valuable than others. In my view, this relationship is not confined to that of student and teacher, but permeates the way in which staff relate to each other. Limiting the group membership to staff or students would not remove the difficulty and to remove power difference from the group would mean that no-one could come. In deliberately choosing to include the word feminist in the title and in resisting the publicly recognized marks of authority, we make ourselves vulnerable to derision and dismissal by the institution. However, the outcome of the group and the research have shown that this vulnerability is also its strength, as Louise Morley and Val Walsh say when referring to the work of feminist academics:

So, whilst feminists can make themselves more vulnerable by drawing attention to themselves as women in the academy, we are paradoxically strengthened for being part of a wider political movement for change. (Morley and Walsh, 1995, p. 3)

My own view of feminist work is that it recognizes and celebrates individual difference, validates individuals' lived experience, recognizes power inequality and actively seeks to minimize it and to offer the power of privilege as a positive resource to others. These are the values I have tried to work to.

What we are trying to do is to create a feminist space in the academy in two hours each month with an ever-changing group of women. We are not simply swimming against the tide, we are attempting to create a subversive discourse within the establishment; one which encourages collaboration, creativity, support and constructive criticism and a respect for our emotional, personal and spiritual lives as well as our intellectual abilities. Kate Campbell writes about the way in which feminism has been incorporated by the academy: '. . . building it up and replenishing it in some ways, yes; but at the same time given to running it dry, keeping it within walls, seeing to its overall containment' (Campbell, 1992, p. 2). The space which we have tried to create is one which allows and encourages connection between self and work, emotion and cognition (Griffin, 1978). We have shared pain and laughter, anger and excitement and challenged some of the norms of competition and patronage. Our attempt to do something different means that each meeting is an adventure where we have to try to negotiate the differences between us in a productive way (Lorde, 1984) and sometimes this works better than other times. It can be hard to acknowledge feelings of confusion and inadequacy in front of someone whose work you supervise, or vice versa, and at times the discomfort shows itself in laughter or defensiveness. I expect it will always be difficult to stay open because the energy and time that women have left for actively creating such a supportive environment is limited. The demands on many women are considerable, arising from the 'double burden' of combining work with domestic responsibilities and also from the way in which, in a patriarchal culture, women are expected to carry a larger share of pastoral and administrative responsibilities (Morley, 1995). In commenting on the group one woman echoed this:

> I think this is an excellent, even crucial support for feminist research and am delighted that it is being done and that *I am not responsible*. (my emphasis)

We have resolved as a group that we will support the work of individuals and not become another institution which puts pressure on members, and so we have adopted principles of maximizing accessibility. Women from all levels and all aspects of the university's work are welcome and there is no pressure on women to attend. This is quite different from the usual format for research groups in the institution, which invite 'high profile' speakers and act as an arena for individuals to demonstrate and be questioned on their expertise. In our group women are entitled to self-define as feminist and can take part in the group without needing to demonstrate research 'activity' or visibility. An interest in feminist work is enough.

It is now over a year since the initial idea for the group. My own perception of it is that it is a success. I no longer feel the sense of isolation and marginalization in my work. I have a sense of being part of a group of feminists in academia which not only supports my work but also challenges me to take it seriously. The issue of power relationships is one which I think we will continue to struggle with and which will limit the freedom of discussion and even attendance for some women. However, attendance at meetings has continued to be from women across the range of staff and students and the process of the group meetings is one which promotes a degree of equality. The established group norm that, in the first part of the meeting we bring 'ourselves' sharing information and feelings about our work and its context in our lives has the effect of making connections between us and reducing the importance of institutional status, welcoming and making space for new comers and discouraging the forming of a sub- group or clique of 'regulars'. Making ourselves vulnerable in this way is a key aspect of our efforts to maintain a feminist process as well as content to the discussions and has made it more possible for individuals to bring their puzzles and ideas about their work rather than a prepared paper.

Avril Butler

The cross-disciplinary membership, not restricted to teaching staff, means that our common starting point is our feminism and that we have something to contribute to each others' work whatever discipline it is within. The emphasis on feminist practice is highlighted by the group member who said:

> There is a need for me to connect with other women with a feminist agenda [it] feeds my resistance and enables my survival in academia; ensures continued connection between feminist theory and practice for me, here and now.

Reflections

The fact of writing and presenting this paper has clarified for me the importance of someone acting as a coordinator for the group who has access to the 'hidden resources' of photocopying, postage, financial security and travel expenses for conferences for example. It feels consistent with my feminist values to use my position to support a feminist space in the academy through convening and servicing the group, recording its achievements and making them public. This conflicts at times with my wish that the responsibility and ownership of the group could be fully and equally shared, but without the work of a consistent convenor and secretary I think it is unlikely that the group would have continued because of the demands on women's time and energy. Producing the paper has acted as a way of validating the group and raising the profile of feminist research within the institution. It has also clarified and made explicit some of the principles for the group and can be used for introducing the group to new members. I am, however, conscious of the tension between this improved clarity and visibility for the group and the risk of our falling into traditional patterns or becoming fixed in a dogmatic way of working. We need to maintain feminist praxis, which Gaby Weiner describes as: '. . . being continually subject to revision as a result of experience, reflexive and self-reflexive, widely accessible and open to change, explicitly political and value-led' (Weiner, 1995, p. 130). I trust that the values we hold will enable us to continue to be reflexive and open to change and that we will consistently re-make the group as we go along in response to the changing needs of feminists in higher education.

References

BUTLER, A. and LANDELLS, M. (1994) *Telling Tales out of School: Research into Sexual Harassment of Women Academics*, Plymouth: University of Plymouth.
BUTLER, S. and WINTRAM, C. (1991) *Feminist Groupwork,* London: Sage.
CAMPBELL, K. (ed.) (1992) 'Introduction: Matters of theory and practice — or, we'll be coming out the harbour', in *Critical Feminism: Argument in the Disciplines*, Buckingham: Open University Press.
COLLINS, P. (1991) *Black Feminist Thought: Knowledge, Consciousness and the Politics of Empowerment*, New York: Routledge.

DAVIS, L.V. (ed.) (1994) *Building on Women's Strengths: A Social Work Agenda for the Twenty-first Century*, New York: The Haworth Press.

DU BOIS, B. (1983) 'Passionate scholarship: Notes on values, knowing and method in feminist social science', in BOWLES, G. and DUELLI KLEIN, R. (eds) *Theories of Women's Studies*, London: Routledge and Kegan Paul, pp. 105–17.

ERNST, S. and GOODISON, L. (1993) *In Our Own Hands: A Book of Self-help Therapy*, London: The Women's Press.

FUENTES, C.R. (1996) 'Todas locas, todas vivas, todas libres': Chilean lesbians 1980–95', in REINFELDER, M. (ed.) *Amazon to Zami: Towards a Global Lesbian Feminism*, London: Cassell.

GOTTLIEB, N., BURDEN, D., McCORMICK, R. and NICARTHY, G. (1983) 'The distinctive attributes of feminist groups', in GLOVER REED, B. and GARVIN, C.D. (eds) 'Groupwork with women/groupwork with men: An overview of gender issues in social groupwork practice', *Social Work with Groups: A Journal of Community and Clinical Practice*, **6**, 3/4, New York: The Haworth Press, pp. 81–93.

GRIFFIN, S. (1978) *Woman and Nature: The Roaring Inside Her*, New York: Harper and Row.

HUMM, M. (1991) ' "Thinking of things in themselves": Theory, experience, women's studies,' in AARON, J. and WALBY, S. (eds) *Out of the Margins: Women's Studies on the 90s*, London: Falmer Press, pp. 49–62.

LIBRERIA DELLE DONNE DI MILANO (1991) 'More women than men,' in BONO, P. and KEMP, S. (eds) *Italian Feminist Thought: A Reader*, Oxford: Basil Blackwell.

LORDE, A. (1984) 'The master's tools will never dismantle the master's house,' in *Sister Outsider*, Freedom: The Crossing Press, pp. 110–11.

MORLEY, L. (1994) 'Glass ceiling or iron cage: Women in UK academia', in *Gender, Work and Organization*, **1**, 4, Oxford: Basil Blackwell, pp. 194–204.

MORLEY, L. (1995) 'An agenda for gender: Women in the university', in *The European Journal of Women's Studies*, vol. **2**, London: Sage, pp. 271–5.

MORLEY, L. and WALSH, V. (eds) (1995) *Feminist Academics: Creative Agents for Change*, London: Taylor and Francis.

RAMAZANOGLU, C. (1987) 'Sex and violence in academic life or you can keep a good woman down,' in HANMER, J. and MAYNARD, M. (eds) *Women, Violence and Social Control*, Basingstoke: Macmillan.

RAYMOND, J. (1996) *A Passion for Friends: Towards a Philosophy of Female Affection*, London: Women's Press.

STEINEM, G. (1992) 'Helping ourselves to revolution', *MS*, **111**, 3, November/December.

WEINER, G. (1995) *Feminisms in Education*, Basingstoke: Open University Press.

WHITAKER STOCK, D. (1985) *Using Groups to Help People*, London: Routledge and Kegan Paul.

10   Women and Collective Action: The Role of the Trade Union in Academic Life

Ann J. Kettle

Introduction: The Road to Activism

Inspired by one of the WHEN 1996 conference themes — 'working with women/ working for women' — I began to think about my own lengthy experience as a female academic and about how far I had worked either with women or for women over the past 30 years. I am a medieval historian by trade and this process of reflection reminded me of the opening of Christine de Pizan's *Book of the City of Ladies* (written in 1406). Christine was, if not the first feminist, the first female historian and the first woman to attempt to defend her own sex against the near universal misogyny of the Middle Ages. Sitting in her study she reflects that she cannot recognize herself or the women she knows in the misogynist tract that she is reading. She then sets about building, with the help of three crowned ladies, Reason, Rectitude and Justice, the City of Ladies, a refuge for virtuous women against the attacks of men — an early example of female collective action. Over 500 years later I feel that my own experience has some similarities with that of Christine. I have been inspired by injustice and discrimination to begin working with women and for women and that involvement has enriched my career and changed its direction.

There is an expanding literature on women's participation in higher education as students, teachers and researchers (Adams, 1996; Dyhouse, 1995; Davies, Quinn and Lubelska, 1994; Griffiths, 1996) but although some research has been undertaken on the role of women in trade unions (Lawrence, 1994) little of it has been specific to higher education. This is therefore necessarily a very personal account of the place of trade union activity in an academic career and the necessity of collective action to improve the position of women in higher education. The first member of my family to attend university, I went to Oxford in the late 1950s where I was outnumbered nine to one by males. I was, of course, a member of an all-female college and I distinctly remember being berated by an elderly female don for not wearing my gown — 'We fought for your right to wear a gown'. My only experience of collective action as an undergraduate was organizing a petition against the disgusting college food. After graduating and a spell of postgraduate research (my supervisor did not approve of doctorates, even for 'gentlemen'), I found a post as, what would now be called, a contract research worker — a suitable job for a woman. I was then fortunate to obtain a university lectureship at a time of expansion when there were sufficient jobs available to take a risk on a woman ('how useful to have a woman in the department').

Throughout over 30 years as a university teacher I have frequently felt conscious of being a woman in a male-dominated profession: the only woman on Senate ('Miss Kettle and gentlemen') and the first woman faculty officer (I had to be made an honorary man because the secretarial staff worked for 'the men' and couldn't cope with a woman 'boss'). I have felt alienated by the pub and sport culture of my male colleagues and have become impatient of arrogant young men. At best I have been patronized: 'haven't you done well for a woman'. At worst I have been sub-jected to abuse: it was suggested, for example, that my promotion came through influence rather than merit and that my courses were popular because they were too easy or, when I began to teach the history of women, not academically respectable. It has been assumed that I am primarily a teacher and I have been denied research leave on the grounds that my male colleagues had their careers to make. But I have stayed on the ladder, only to reach the glass ceiling. Many of my female colleagues have fallen off. Women have retired, often prematurely, and have not been replaced, women have taken voluntary severance, women have left when their contracts came to an end or just left because it was too difficult to combine the demands of family life with an academic career. This may sound like self-pity to younger colleagues but will be only too familiar to women academics of my own vintage.

I was eventually spurred into action by the unashamed paternalism and barely concealed misogyny of my colleagues. When I began my career female academics were a rarity. This was the era of the Robbins Report (1963, p. 193) which painted this picture of the typical university teacher:

> The fact that the colleges own many houses in the near neighbourhood makes it possible for a non-resident tutor to dine in college and be available outside 'office hours' without feeling he is neglecting his wife and family, and he can entertain his students without imposing undue burdens on his wife.

In Scotland in the 1960s if colleagues in the same department married, the woman had to change to a temporary contract; childbirth had either to be timed for the long vacation or combined with 'study leave'; professors stipulated applications only from males in order to save women the trouble of applying for jobs which they were never going to get. Although I had been a member of the Association of University Teachers (AUT) from 1964 it did not occur to me that these were matters for collective action. Indeed the AUT did not become a 'proper' trade union until 1976 (Stuttard, 1992). I remember writing an article (long lost) for the staff newsletter entitled 'The First Blast of the Trumpet' — an unsubtle reference to John Knox and his monstrous regiment of women. This article was about the oddities of life in St Andrews for a female academic and had the effect of marking me out as a dangerous feminist and probably a trouble maker. In common, how-ever, with most of my colleagues, both male and female, I spent the 1970s coping with a heavy burden of teaching, trying to get out publications and becoming increasingly involved in faculty administration.

The funding crisis which began in 1981 with its threat to colleagues' jobs turned me into a trade union activist and my involvement with 'women's issues' followed a few years later. In 1984 I founded a staff women's group, loosely attached to the AUT local association, which has over the years assumed various forms and which still continues to meet irregularly. Through the AUT locally I have been involved in pressing for, and negotiating with the university on such matters as, improved maternity leave, paternity and adoptive leave, a policy of gender neutral language, an appraisal scheme that provided for women to be trained as appraisers and allowed women to choose to be appraised by women, the recognition of gender inequalities in discretionary pay, etc. Most of these issues were subsumed in an equal opportunities policy which was negotiated in 1991. Since then our efforts locally have been concentrated on refining this policy and trying to get it properly implemented. Outside St Andrews I was a member of AUT's national women's committee between 1990 and 1994 and as president of AUT (Scotland) I organized a conference on equal opportunities in Edinburgh in 1995. I also chair an advisory group for a Scottish Higher Education Funding Council initiative designed to increase the numbers of women in science, engineering and technology in Scottish universities.

Equal Opportunities and the Need for Collective Action

My own experience of slow awakening, growing frustration and then hectic involvement reveals the difficulty of organizing women academics. The energies of the women who have made it into the profession tend to be concentrated on preserving their jobs and establishing themselves within their own disciplines. In my experience the demands of teaching and research, and the pastoral work at which women are thought to be so good, leave little time for collective action. Recently, the rapid expansion of student numbers, and the twin pressures of quality assessment of teaching and research have left women with even less time or energy for collective action. The AUT survey, *Long Hours, Little Thanks* (AUT, 1994) showed that women academics, particularly those in promoted posts, were working longer hours than their male colleagues. One response to this survey (Hobsbaum, 1994, p. 8) pointed out that, 'The university is an institution devised by men, run by men, and still catering primarily for men.'

The facts and figures of discrimination against women working in higher education are well known and do not need elaboration. In 1978 AUT's newly established equal opportunities working party reported that women academics made up only 11 per cent of university staff and that they were disproportionately concentrated in the lower grades; only 13 per cent of women were above lecturer grade, compared with 34 per cent of men (Stuttard, 1992). Although the proportion of female professors improved slightly from 1.8 per cent in 1972 to 2.7 per cent in 1979, the proportion of women in promoted posts actually declined during the 1970s (Rendel, 1984). In the 1993–4 academic year women comprised 21.2 per cent of all academic staff compared to 12.8 per cent in 1983–4 (AUT, 1995). The proportion of female professors has slowly inched up from 3.1 per cent in 1988 (CVCP, 1991) to 7.3 per cent in 1995 (*Times Higher*, 1996). As was pointed out in 1990 (Halsey, 1990) the reasons for the unequal distribution of women between subjects and grades are unclear and 'open to further enquiry and, no doubt, protracted, dispute'. The figures do, however, reveal the slowness of the progress towards equality of opportunity for women academics in higher education.

Equal opportunities are of central importance at all stages of the careers of women working in higher education. First comes access or getting a job, with issues involving recruitment: advertising, application forms, selection for interview, interviewing procedures and selection criteria. Access is followed by participation with issues involving conditions of employment: probation, training and staff development, child care, family leave, flexible working, grievance and disciplinary procedures. Finally there is progression which should involve equal opportunities in promotion procedures. All these matters should be included in equal opportunities policies. In 1991 the Committee of Vice-Chancellors and Principals issued guidance on *Equal Opportunities in Employment in Universities*, prompted more perhaps by concern about the legal consequences of discrimination in employment practices than by the desire for equality of treatment. But this concern has led to the establishment of equal opportunities policies in most universities and the appointment of equal opportunities officers in some institutions. In 1993 the Commission on University Career Opportunity (CUCO) was established by the CVCP with an impressive mission statement (CUCO, 1994, p. 3):

> The Commission will use publicity and persuasion to help universities to ensure that staff in all modes of employment are fairly selected, deployed, appraised, developed, rewarded, promoted and otherwise fairly treated.

Publicity, persuasion and guidance on good practice (Farish, McPake, Powney and Weiner, 1995) cannot in themselves produce equality of opportunity and the trade union has a crucial role to play in ensuring the implementation of equal opportunity policies. In view of the pressures on individual women and the limited concerns of managements only the trade union can offer the necessary collective action on policy matters and provide the help and support needed by individual women fighting discrimination.

Forms of Collective Action

Women have the opportunity to participate in collective action in various ways and at different levels. At the national level AUT began to be concerned with equal opportunities in the late 1970s. An equal opportunities workshop held in 1982 and crowded with members from nearly every university in the country resulted in a 'major change' in the Association (Stuttard, 1992) with the establishment of an annual national meeting for women members and a national women's committee. The women's committee has operated as a very effective pressure group within the trade union. With the help of the annual meeting it has been responsible for the formation of AUT's policies on a wide range of equal opportunities issues, including widowers' pensions, age discrimination, gender neutral language, anonymous marking, parental and carers' leave, sexual harassment and consensual relationships between staff and students. The committee also organizes training and workshop sessions for women members and produces each year three issues of a newsheet, *AUT WOMAN* which is distributed to all members of the Association. As a federal organization AUT has to rely on its local associations for the implementation of its policies and locally success with 'women's issues' tends to depend on the extent of female involvement in union activities such as negotiating committees and the handling of personal cases. Many women, myself included, have become active at national level through membership of local association committees.

The most informal organization is a staff women's group which in my experience can be a very valuable way of providing support, sharing experiences and promoting friendships among female colleagues. Many women are still isolated in their departments or laboratories and welcome the opportunity to gossip and exchange information once they have overcome their suspicion that the group is the preserve of feminists and union activists. Although women's groups are not usually confined exclusively to union members, they can also be a useful way of introducing women to the benefits of collective action and can operate as effective informal networks and pressure groups in the establishment and implementation of equal opportunities policies.

Tensions, Frustrations and Rewards

The opportunities for collective action by women and for women do exist but there are undoubtedly tensions which often prevent them from operating as effectively as they might. Compared to other unions women members of AUT are more actively involved: in 1988 despite women making up only 15 per cent of the membership, 19 per cent of that membership attended council and 21 per cent of the national executive were women (AUT, 1989). Yet there is still a resistance by women in higher education first to join their unions and then become involved in collective action. This may simply be the result of lack of time or possibly in some cases a deep seated belief born of bitter experience in the virtues of self-sufficiency; the latter attitude is exemplified by survival guides such as Laura Caplan's (1993). Possibly some women see collective action on employment matters as inappropriate to academic life and perhaps trade unions are seen by some as traditional male preserves. As Laurel Brake pointed out (AUT, 1988, p. 1):

> In addition the confrontational way in which negotiations take place locally and the way in which trade union policy is made by motions, resolutions and formal debate in council can intimidate and alienate women. Aware of this problem the women's committee drew up a 'user's guide' to council and was responsible for the introduction of non-resolutionary business to help facilitate the free exchange

of ideas and opinions outside the normal framework of council business. It must, however, be admitted that, in spite of the civilising efforts of women, there are still some unreconstructed male activists who are easily identified by the excessive length of their speeches and their resistance to 'politically correct' language.

Equal opportunities issues can be a source of tension within the trade union both locally and nationally. They are seen as a distraction from the primary business of a trade union which is the protection of members' jobs and negotiations on pay. It is perhaps significant that equal opportunities is a comparative newcomer on the AUT agenda and only figures at the top of that agenda when there is no more pressing business or when equal opportunities can be linked to a pay claim. By means of a curious double bind equal opportunities have been seen both as a matter for women activists to deal with but also as not exclusively concerning women, since issues of sexual orientation, race and disability are also involved. When women were awarded 'specialist group' status within AUT's national organization there was considerable debate at local and national level on whether it was really necessary to have some form of separate organization to consider women's questions (Stuttard, 1992). The presence of women activists in the other specialist groups, i.e. librarians, administrative, computing and contract research staff, can lead to complaints about the privileging of women's concerns.

Tensions at national level are reflected at local level where there can be found the same complaints about undue concentration on 'women's issues', coupled with a willingness to jump on the equal opportunities bandwagon when convenient. Many of the issues associated with equal opportunities are both contentious and ambiguous. This can be illustrated by the matters over which I first became active. It was men who were the main beneficiaries of the campaign for widowers' pensions. The issue of gender neutral language was seen by both male and female colleagues as at best a pointless waste of time and at worst as a distortion of the English language. The proposal to introduce the anonymous marking of examination scripts was vigorously opposed by male colleagues who saw it as a fundamental attack on professional standards but who now accept it as good practice and even welcome it as a protection against charges of partiality.

Pressure from the union for the implementation of equal opportunities policies can cause divisions among members. In spite of paying lip service to the principle of equal opportunity, university managements are wary of attracting charges of positive discrimination and are reluctant to set targets for the recruitment and promotion of women which they know are unlikely to be met. Attempts by the union to ensure equal opportunities in selection and promotion can be seen as potentially depriving men of jobs and advancement. Maternity leave, the only condition of service which is exclusively female, has been broadened into parental or family responsibility leave and the campaign for child care on campus has been to the benefit of both women staff and fathers with working partners. The most contentious area, however, has been that of sexual harassment and the allied issue of consensual relationships between staff and students. At the prompting of the unions and in order to avoid expensive legal action universities have put in place procedures for dealing with charges of sexual and racial harassment and many have established networks of advisers (mainly women) to deal informally with complaints of harassment. Union involvement in such matters causes resentment among male colleagues who often claim that they have only joined in order to secure protection against charges of sexual harassment. Women can be disillusioned when it becomes clear that management are not primarily concerned with the harassment of students by staff and that serious cases are either hushed up or dealt with through high level disciplinary procedures (AUT, 1991; AUT, 1995). Attempts to introduce codes of practice on consensual relationships between staff and students have been seen as an intolerable invasion of private life rather than an attempt to impose professional standards of behaviour (Carter and Jeffs, 1995). Recently AUT policy on the issue of abuse of power which is at the root of sexual harassment has been broadened to include procedures for dealing with bullying (AUT, 1995).

Attempts at collective action can also reveal differing attitudes among women and can accentuate the differences between women working in higher education. There is no longer one simple stereotype of the academic woman: the blue stocking spinster, entirely devoted to her subject and her pupils to the exclusion of a private life. In addition to divisions based on class, race, sexuality, etc., there are distinctions between young and old, between those on permanent and those on temporary contracts, between those with children and those without, between those who are too timid to seek help and those who are securely established in their careers and do not see why women should need any special help or protection.

The fact remains that universities have one of the lowest proportions of senior women employees of all the professions. I recently ran a workshop for AUT's annual women's meeting on 'Strategies for Advancement'. We did not reach strategies for getting promoted because the majority of the women taking part were on short-term contracts with no possibility of promotion. The scarcity of women in promoted posts in universities is, however, difficult to explain on grounds of simple discrimination alone. Gender differences such as the different career patterns of men and women, the absence of child care facilities or role models, women's lack of mobility or reluctance to outshine husband or partners must also be taken into account. Women are perhaps socialized to despise in themselves and other women the self-advertisement which is now a necessary part of a successful academic career (AUT, 1993).

The furore in Oxford in 1993 over the proposal to create 15 new professorships, a move partly prompted by the proliferation of so-called 'mickey mouse' chairs in the new universities, highlighted the dilemma faced by women academics. A victorious counter proposal suggested that a larger number of readerships should instead be created in order to give women a fairer chance of promotion. This row produced some predictable press speculation: 'Are women simply not up to the academic mark?' (*The Times*, 1993) and 'Are women too self-effacing?' (*Times Higher*, 1993). These gender differences have surfaced again in the 'transfer market' created by the 1996 research assessment exercise. It has been argued that not only has the research assessment exercise increased inequality between men and women but also between 'conventional' women academics who struggle to balance teaching and research with family responsibilities and a breed of 'new academic women' who are able to compete with and even outplay their male colleagues (correspondence in *Times Higher*, 1995).

The 'new academic woman' has also made an appearance in the correspondence columns of *AUT WOMAN* (spring 1996, p. 2, summer 1996, p. 2). A male academic accused *AUT WOMAN* of crying 'foul' when women:

> who recognise that, as human beings, they have roles as home-makers, child-bearers and child-rearers, do not achieve professorial status at the same rate as do men . . . Leaving one's babies and toddlers to be looked after by strangers may be a prudent policy for a woman academic eager to achieve promotion. But is it good for the children?

A female contributor to the debate identified the characteristics of the newest sort of academic women:

> They may or may not have academic abilities, but they attend assertiveness courses, participate in women-only organisations, spend a large proportion of their salary buying designer clothes, and use the male gender to their advantage. Their husbands, or rather partners, (as marriage is outdated in their opinion) must wash their own clothes, shop and cook the meals and baby-sit for 'women nights out'.

Fortunately, the letter continues, universities maintain a sensible, lower percentage of female academics than female undergraduates and the few 'new women' tend to be avoided by staff and students and thought of as 'peculiar'. The attempt to identify the characteristics of the 'new' academic woman has clearly exposed some raw nerves and the debate has highlighted the difficult choices which face women in academic life as well as the discrimination and prejudice which still exist.

There are certainly frustrations involved in working for women. Ensuring that equal opportunities policies are observed can be time consuming; there are too few women available to sit on selection committees as 'statutory skirts', 'show girls' or 'watch bitches'; the very names used show the irony with which such an essential activity is often regarded even by women. The effective operation of trade union activities depends on voluntary labour by those who often have the least time to spare and who are vulnerable to exploitation (AUT, 1988). There is understandable irritation as each new batch of activists discovers women's issues and begins to re-invent the wheel. In the post-feminist age of the 'new academic woman' there can be considerable resistance to the idea that collective action is still necessary.

There are, however, considerable rewards in the form of new friends and networks outside one's own institution or professional circles and great satisfaction to be gained from the successful outcome of a personal case. I was much encouraged when a colleague at another university told me that I had 'spoken to her condition' in an article which I had written for *AUT WOMAN* (AUT, 1993) on the gender issues surrounding promotion. In spite of the tensions involved women do still need organizing and the most effective way to do this is through trade union activity, nationally and locally. Women need be more confident of their ability to

Ann J. Kettle

improve their position and that of their female colleagues through collective action. They should press for the proper implementation and monitoring of their institution's equal opportunities policy. They should, through their unions, encourage their institutions to set targets for the appointment and promotion of women and to take positive action to achieve those targets. Collective action by women will not solve all the problems and dilemmas faced by women in higher education but it should at the very least result in more academic women, of whatever variety.

References

ADAMS, P. (1996) *Somerville for Women: An Oxford College 1879–1993*, Oxford: Oxford University Press.

AUT (1994) *Long Hours, Little Thanks: A Survey of the Use of Time by Full-time Academic and Related Staff in the Traditional University*, London: AUT.

AUT (1995) *Dealing with Harassment: A Guide to Handling Complaints*, London: AUT.

AUT WOMAN (1988) Activism and exploitiaion, Summer, 14, London: AUT.

AUT WOMAN (1989) Women in unions, Autumn, 18, London: AUT.

AUT WOMAN (1991) Sexual harassment in UK universities, Autumn, 24, London: AUT.

AUT WOMAN (1993) 'Serpents and ladders: gender issues in promotion and discretionary pay', Autumn, 30, London: AUT.

AUT WOMAN (1995) 'Paying the price: sexual harassment in higher education', Spring, 34, London: AUT.

AUT WOMAN (1995) 'Position of women academic staff improving slowly', Autumn, 36, London: AUT.

AUT WOMAN (1996) 'Letters', Spring, 37, London: AUT.

AUT WOMAN (1996) 'Letters', Summer, 38, London: AUT.

CAPLAN, P.J. (1993) *Lifting a Ton of Feathers: A Woman's Guide to Surviving in the Academic World*, Toronto: University of Toronto Press.

CARTER, P. and JEFFS, T. (1995) *A Very Private Affair: Sexual Exploitation in Higher Education*, Ticknall: Education Now Books.

CUCO (1994) *A Report on Universities' Policies and Practices on Equal Opportunities in Employment*, London: CVCP.

CVCP (1991) *Equal Opportunities in Employment in Universities*, London: CVCP.

DAVIES, S., QUINN, J. and LUBELSKA, C. (eds) (1994) *Changing the Subject: Women in Higher Education*, London: Taylor and Francis.

DYHOUSE, C. (1995) *No Distinction of Sex? Women in British Universities 1870–1939*, London: UCL Press.

FARISH, M., McPAKE, J., POWNEY, J. and WEINER, G. (1995) *Equal Opportunties in Colleges and Universities: Towards Better Practices*, Buckingham: SRHE and Open University Press.

GRIFFITHS, S. (ed.) (1996) *Beyond the Glass Ceiling: Forty Women Whose Ideas Shape the Modern World*, Manchester: Manchester University Press.

HALSEY, A.T. (1990) 'The long, open road to equality', *Times Higher Education Supplement*, 9 February, p. 17.

HOBSBAUM, P. (1994) 'System that sends female academics to an early grave', *Sunday Times*, 30 October, p. 8.

LAWRENCE, E. (1994) *Gender and Trade Unions*, London: Taylor and Francis.

PIZAN, C. DE (1406) *The Book of the City of Ladies*, RICHARDS, E.J. (trans.) (1982), New York: Persea Books.

RENDEL, M. (1984) 'Women academics in the seventies', in ACKER, S. and PIPER, D.W. (eds) *Is Higher Education Fair to Women?*, Guildford: SRHE and NFER-Nelson.

THE ROBBINS REPORT (1963) *Report of the Committee on Higher Education*, Cmnd. 2154, London: HMSO.

STUTTARD, G. (1992) *The Crisis Years: The History of the Association of University Teachers from 1969 to 1983*, London: AUT.

11 Who Goes There, Friend or Foe? Black Women, White Women and Friendships in Academia

Sonia Thompson

Introduction

> Much feminist theory emerges from privileged women who live at the center,
> whose perspectives on reality rarely include knowledge and awareness of the lives
> of women who live on the margin. . . . At its most visionary, it [feminist theory]
> will emerge from individuals who have knowledge of both margin and center.
> (hooks, 1984, preface)

When bell hooks wrote about the centre and the margins of life she was referring
to her own experiences and those of other black people who lived in segregated
America. They knew only too well the two faces of American society. As carriers
of water and hewers of wood, they were at the centre of society, providing services
for their white masters and mistresses. This situation made them intimately aware
of the opportunities and resources that were denied them because of 'race'. Thus
African-Americans were both centred and marginalized people. This chapter has
provided me with the occasion as a black woman to reflect upon my own experiences of a centred and marginalized life in British academia.

hooks' title, *Feminist-Theory from Margin to Center*, reflects the problems
that black women have and continue to face when attempting to take their rightful
place at the core of ideas about women's lives, theories about women's oppression,
and strategies for confronting subjugation.

One of the reasons why I am writing this chapter is to speak to other black
women in academia, because our minority status is such an isolating experience. It
is also an opportunity to make my own voice heard, and to do so without interruption from those who have other agendas in mind. Finally, this chapter is a space to
consider the issue of friendships between white and black women, and to ask
whether such things are possible, given differential power relations and the incredibly competitive environment of higher education.

Division is without doubt one of the major threats to feminism. The women's
movement has been embroiled in debate about its own capacity to deal with difference, in particular differences between white women and black women (Lorde,
1979). The lack of discussion in other areas including disability could be said to be

part of a wider problem of exclusion, which black women have begun to address by forcing the issue of 'race' onto the agenda. I aim to consider some of these differences within the wider context of the academy. The chapter therefore begins by reflecting on some of my own lived experiences as a black woman lecturer within higher education. This will offer an opening to highlight some of the differences in experience between black and white women academics. I also wish to consider how white women have responded to the specific problems that I have encountered within the university environment, and emphasize some issues which are more specific to the unequal power relations between black women and white women in the academy. Thus questions are raised about the prospect of favourable relationships between feminist theories and feminist practices. I write this chapter as a black woman who has worked in higher education on a full-time basis for over eight years. My professional life has been characterized by cultural and ethnic isolation, consequently my experiences can only be written from that perspective. I have occasionally been able to unite with other women within academia and some of those links have been across the colour-divide. It is those relationships (some of which have been positive, but the overwhelming majority have not), which have shaped the way that I have criticized and continue to be able to conceive of the need and possibility of a social relationship with white women feminists.

Personal and Political Values

Omolade's statement that 'no institution of "higher learning" and few publications and magazines allowed the black woman to speak and write her story in her own way' (1994, p. 109) remains valid today. In reflecting on my own experiences, I also draw inspiration from Bryan, Dadzie and Scafe (1985). They argue the need for black women to tell their own herstories, and to assign them to print. Consequently the chapter will not be overburdened by traditional academic referencing. Where possible I make use of writings by other black women in higher education, and draw from their experiences. Although much of this material is American in origin, it is surprisingly relevant, and operates to impress upon the reader the uniformity of gendered-racism in academia. Details of the 'daily humiliations' (Fulani, 1988, p. xvi) of everyday racism and sexism which fashion gendered-racism (Essed, 1991) will provide the backdrop to discuss some of the social interactions I encounter with white women staff within higher education. Black women and white women come to their gender realities though 'different doors'. This shapes their relations in society, the organization and thus, their day-to-day relationships with each other. But if this is a common, even shared dilemma:

> Do others feel as I do? Do you too come to the women's world from a different direction, on a different level, chasing different devils? It is not that I or my friends do not want to be part of the issues which concern other women. Our problems are different but the same. We know the strength and comfort to be found in the company of women. (Pat, 1986, p. 45)

I chose to include this statement by a disabled woman as a reminder to myself and others that whilst womanhood bands us together, it is our differences within that commonality which threaten to disperse us. Like the woman who wrote this piece I feel the need to highlight both the differences and similarities between myself and others (in this case white women). Whilst my experience of womanhood is different, it is at the same time comparable to that which others experience. The opening statement is powerful, because it also aptly illustrates some of the misunderstandings between black and white women. It highlights the point that 'difference' has historically been used as a euphemism for inferiority.

> Women of color, lesbians, and poor and working-class women always knew they were different from white heterosexual middle-class women, and that their differences made them socially inferior and subordinate to that group. Conversely, white heterosexual middle-class women took advantage of the privilege of their superior position to marginalize and oppress other women. (McKay, 1993, p. 272)

Recognizing the complexity of black women's situation is an essential element of the movement towards feminist alliances. Essed (1991) draws attention to the idea that black women experience a form of racism which is qualitatively different from black men. Utilizing an analogy from metallurgy, we note that bronze is made from the amalgamation of two metals, tin and copper. So whilst bronze shares many of the features of each of its constituent metals, it makes up a new alloy altogether, with new characteristics that neither share. Essed has named this combined form of oppression gendered-racism to distinguish its underlying features. In this way it is possible to conceptualize at a deeper level the ways in which black women are exposed to a particular form of racism. For example, racially harassed black women are vulnerable to a form of persecution which hinges on their gender position in society. Many Asian women in the East End of London are routinely racially harassed as they walk their children to and from school (Wilson, 1978). The physical and verbal harassment is made all the more powerful because it revolves around exploiting women's physical vulnerability.

It follows, that if black women experience gendered-racism, then they must also experience racialized-sexism. One of the many images of women of African descent is that of the sexually experienced woman with a voracious appetite for men (Bell Scott, 1982) (never for other women). Such women are not seen as candidates for rape. Racialized-sexism calls into question the extent to which African women can gain access to justice following acts of sexual abuse.

Pat's (1986) statement finally serves as a salutary reminder that I write as a woman within a middle-class agency dominated not only by whiteness and maleness, but also by the norms of non-disabledness and heterosexuality. Although this chapter concentrates on the possibility and experience of friendships between black and white women, some women are oppressed in these and other ways. Such a political overview demands work on my own values, attitudes, and behaviours towards women who also come to their woman-ness from 'another route'.

My Own Experiences: Organizational Culture and Context

Friendships rely on sharing, building trust and taking risks, sometimes without knowing when you are likely to receive something in return. The organizational culture of the academy by contrast is characterized by the cut and thrust of debate, and intense rivalry for ever-dwindling resources. At an address to a Barnard college audience, Toni Morrison made the following comment:

> I am alarmed at the violence that women do to each other; professional violence, competitive violence, emotional violence. I am alarmed by a growing absence of decency in the killing floor of professional women's world. (Toni Morrison, May 1979, cited in hooks, 1984, p. 49)

Working in an adversarial and hostile atmosphere is damaging for all women, but not I would argue, equally so. Organizational culture in practice often means fitting in with the organization, dropping out or being pushed. Sexism, racism, competition and friendship are not easy bedfellows, yet it is within this environment that black women academics are expected to build friendships and to survive.

There is evidence that senior management has a major impact on organizational culture (Selznick, 1957). By organizational culture I mean the agency's 'prevailing patterns of values, attitudes, beliefs, assumptions, expectations, activities, interactions, norms and sentiments' (French and Bell, 1990). Organizational culture is evasive (Deal and Kennedy, 1983), but the culture of higher education has been and continues to be influenced by those who dominate senior positions, that is white men. Certainly there is little evidence to suggest that black women are being recruited into senior positions in higher education in numbers which reflect the increase in student numbers (Mirza, 1994). This exposes the recent drive to recruit black students to higher education as an economic need to draw on one of the last remaining reserve army of students, rather than a moral desire to extend equal of opportunity.

Black women academics have joined higher education establishments after white women. This means that notions of what constitutes organizational gender issues have already been colonized by white women, who have had longer to make use of existing structures, and to speak with white men on matters which have been deemed 'gender issues'. This certainly does not mean that white women have won the fight on feminism, but that they have a head start on black women, who are being asked to join something which already exists, and thus on white women's terms.

For black women, getting their agendas addressed is an uphill struggle. Jewell (1993) for instance, argues that black women have the least common physical attributes compared with white men in privileged classes. Black women, because of 'race' and gender combined, are also over represented amongst the poor, and so are further away than most groups from being members of the upper class. Women of African descent do, however, share independence, assertion, decisiveness and task-orientation with white men, and as such are a contradiction in gender terms for both white men and white women.

Additionally, I would suggest that where academic staff are not black women, that they tend to compartmentalize 'race' from gender, and assume that all the women are white and all the black people are men. One statement by two academics (Hearn and Parkin, 1987), illustrates just this point. In their book entitled *Sex at Work: The Power and Paradox of Organisation Sexuality*, the authors' use of racism to highlight sexism is an appropriation of the black experience, which does a great deal to exclude black women from a discussion of racist and sexist language. Their statement typifies the simplistic notion of what constitutes gender oppression, and therefore what it means to be a woman.

> Most organisations are havens of sexist language. . . . Imagine how offensive and harassing to black people all the above [sexist and sexually exclusive] words would be if they were routinely changed to read 'white power', 'chair white', 'state white' etc. (Hearn and Parkin, 1987, p. 145)

The reality is that as a black person *and* a woman I am equally horrified by both racist and sexist language. The irony is that Hearn and Parkin (1987) have made the mistake that so many others have, that is to write as if racism and sexism are mutually exclusive experiences. The effect of this approach is to exclude those who are most affected by the issues they have raised. It is disappointing when white men hold these views but it is a corruption of womanhood when white feminists hold and act upon them as well.

Friendships between black women and white women (not only in universities but more generally) have been overshadowed by racism, and the suspicions that black women have about white feminists (hooks, 1984). Firstly, that they will exploit black women to free themselves from sexism, but then ally themselves with white men as mutual oppressors in 'race'. Secondly there is the fear that in the contest for limited resources, white women will capitalize on their racial advantage.

> The Black woman cannot help being cautious of allying herself with a 'privileged competitor'. (Carroll, 1982, p. 119)

Consequently, how I feel about the possibility of deep and meaningful friendships alters over time and with experience. Some days I am full of sisterhood and dwell on the *need* to unite, rather than the *mechanics* of how this will happen. At other times, the sheer accumulation of repeated racism by white people, both male and female, leads me to concentrate on self-preservation alone. The section which follows chronicles some of the ways in which 'race' and gender interact within higher education.

Daily Humiliations: Everyday Gendered-racism

Within five miles of the university site on which I work there are four electoral wards with an ethnic minority population ranging from 24.9 per cent to 45.9 per cent (EORRD, 1994). These numbers are not reflected in the level of staff. Black women staff are disadvantaged within the system. Not only are they a minority in academia — they make up less than a handful of frontline support staff. On this site there are no black women employed as receptionists, administrators, clerks, or word-processor operators. All of these are areas where women traditionally dominate. Only the library and the kitchen currently employ black women support staff.

Of the 95 non-sessional academic staff employed here, only 10 are visibly black (seven are Asian and three African-Caribbean), and of those three black women only one is African-Caribbean — me. If I was to search out the only other full-time African-Caribbean woman working on this site I would have to go to the canteen. Being the lone full-time African-Caribbean woman academic on site has implications which are wearing.

> . . . with the exception of the Black studies and minority programs I never come into contact with another Black woman professor or administrator in my day-to-day activities. This seems to be typical for most of the Black women in similar positions. There is no one to share similar experiences and gain support, no one with whom to identify, no one on whom a Black woman can model herself. It takes a great deal of psychological strength 'just to get through a day', the endless lunches, and meetings in which one is always 'different'. The feeling is much like the exhaustion a foreigner speaking an alien tongue feels at the end of the day. (Carroll, 1982, p. 119)

For me this situation is alleviated by the presence of two other black (Asian) women, one of whom I share a warm relationship with. Nevertheless, there is plenty of evidence to suggest that the cultural image of black women has been constructed by those in power to support racialized systems of oppression which continue to impact on my working life. Black women academics can expect to be subjected to a range of dilemmas which are predicated on myths about their supposed station in life (Mirza, 1994).

There have been major changes to this university since my arrival several years ago, including an immense building expansion programme. With such radical change, I along with many others, have moved site on several occasions. Each move is accompanied by greater chances of not being recognized by gate-keeping staff, for example, in the library, car-park, photocopying centre. I have lost count of the times when I have been asked at meetings whether I am in the right place, or whether I was aware that the lift was for staff only? One wonders when it ceases to be a coincidence that white students are addressed by people entering my lecture wondering why no one is in charge of the class. I would hazard a guess that few white male lecturers have been publicly accused of imitating academic staff and refused access to resources which so many of them take for granted. It is a shaming experience to be confronted with these behaviours, yet the expectation is that the humiliated individual respond in a 'reasoned' way to the degrader. Most of those who have confronted me have suggested that they treat everyone in exactly the same way. Discussions with other academics indicates that support staff have a schema which they use to judge whether or not an individual could be said to be an academic. Black women deviate considerably from this 'norm'.

Following slavery and colonialism black women continued to be required to fill roles in western Europe as factory hands, cleaners and nurses and to carry out other menial tasks (Bryan, Dadzie and Scafe, 1985). These images endure today, so that in situations where black women 'fill occupational positions other than those defined by cultural images . . . [they are deemed to be] in status discrepant positions' (Jewell, 1993, p. 56). Hegemony, Jewell argues, has also been used to instill the idea that certain groups have justly and appropriately gained resources and social power, so that it is no coincidence that high status occupations are defined as white and male. The role of housewife is deemed as suitable for those who are white and female. Unskilled and semi-skilled jobs are the domain of black males, whilst jobs such as home-worker, nurse, cleaner and public sector cooks are appropriately defined as black and female.

> I went early one morning to a University library at 9.00 a.m. not realising it didn't open until 9.30 a.m. . . . the librarian who I know asked me how I had got in. I said the door was open . . . I went back with her to ask the security man why the door was open . . . when he saw me, he said, 'but she's the cleaner'. (Black woman tutor cited in Bailey et al., 1996)

In fact, the idea that black people are not part of the academic community is likely to have underpinned a racist joke which I heard in the staff room. It never occurred to the teller of the story that a black person might be in the staff room. Even more displeasing is the idea that he assumed that no-one would tackle him about the tale whether they were black or white.

Closer to home, several African-Caribbean women who I have worked with as part-time academics have left the university, completely disillusioned and disappointed with higher education. The negative experiences they have had at the hands of resource gate-keepers and students have led to a range of daily humiliations they have not been prepared to put up with. In several cases the deciding factor has been their experience of racism at the hands of white women academics. They are aware that they are entering academia as a reserve army of lecturers, and that as such they are entering the profession when its status and conditions of service are in decline.

Such daily humiliations in higher education can be a debilitating process and stress the importance of support for black women in higher education.

> The middle class African American woman realizes that she is likely to be the ongoing victim of discrimination and that her informal support system will help to counter the negative effects of overt and covert forms of institutional race and gender discrimination. (Lebsock, 1984, cited in Jewell, 1993, pp. 131–77)

Several years ago, when I was the only black lecturer on site, a black woman friend at a neighbouring university advised me to seek out white liberals in the absence of black colleagues. However, a major problem with liberalism is its predisposition to individual explanations, and this has on occasion been the response of white feminist lecturers when faced with problems emanating from a structural plane. The following section explores a number of issues, not least the ways in which white women academics have responded to issues of 'racial' difference.

White Women and Organization

How do white women interpret the daily humiliations of gendered-racism?

> As women we have been taught to either ignore our differences or to view them as causes for separation and suspicion rather than as forces for change. Without community, there is no liberation, only the most vulnerable and temporary armistice between an individual and her oppression. But community must not mean a shedding of our differences, not the pathetic pretence that these differences do not exist. (Lorde, 1984, p. 112)

Lorde's (1984) comment on differences and similarity highlights the danger of neglecting difference between women. Unfortunately the daily humiliations which are part (but not all of the academic experience) have seldom been analysed within higher education at that level. Firstly, ideas about gender for many white women are dominated by an agenda which focuses almost exclusively on similarity. Few have been able, or indeed willing to identify 'race' as a complicating matter in those day-to-day experiences. Instead, explanations have ranged from a misunderstanding on my part, to age and gender. On several occasions discussions initiated on the topic of gendered-racism have been usurped and the issue of 'race' redefined out of the equation.

It is no secret that black women are virtually invisible in academic texts, and courses. The rise in the number of anthologies, and edited texts on black women (Bryan, Dadzie and Scafe, 1985; Hull, Bell Scott and Smith, 1982; James and Busia, 1993; Smith, 1983; Hine, King and Reed, 1995) is testimony of this academic void.

> Women's studies courses . . . focused almost exclusively upon the lives of white women. Black studies, which was much too often male-dominated, also ignored Black women. . . . Because of white women's racism and Black men's sexism, there was no room in either area for a serious consideration of the lives of Black women. And even when they have considered Black women, white women usually have not had the capacity to analyze racial politics and Black culture, and Black men have remained blind (sic) or resistant to the implications of sexual politics in Black women's lives. (Guy-Sheftall, 1993, p. 77)

I have no experience of a black studies course. However, a women's studies course located the experience of lesbian women and black women under the heading 'deviant women'.

Images of black people in general and of black women in particular precede us. The absence of literature by and about the black woman has led to even more derogatory and damaging images. It is because of the dominant views about black women that two competing ideas about the power of African-Caribbean women have potency. The first one is that black women are completely determined by the oppression of wider society and thus are powerless pathetic victims. The second view is that we are overwhelmingly powerful, coming from a historically matriarchal society where we are dominant and domineering super-mammies.

> [W]e are told that Black women, in slavery and afterward, were a formidable people, 'matriarchs', in fact. Rarely has so much power been attributed to so vulnerable a group. (Lebock, 1984, pp. 87–8, cited in Jewell, 1993, p. 131)

Some white women hold both views about black women's power. Hence my own experience of being considered by the same white feminist as incredibly oppressed by black and white men and also by white women. Yet because of this, I was also informed that I was 'too powerful'. Where white women hold such contradictory views, it has been my experience that they have had little lived experience of the black community, nor have they had an active political involvement within it, or close friendships with black women. Their ideas reveal a lack of sophistication of some of the basic ideas about black women's lived circumstances. The reality is that black women are neither pathetic pieces of humanity responding to a never-ending barrage of blows inflicted by their oppressors, nor are they omnipotent beings able to handle every eventuality thrown at them by society. We are mothers and sisters and activists and friends. We have much to offer to each other, to our community and to the world, and as such we can never allow ourselves to be defined by others, because the ideas which others have about who and what we are, are so very limiting.

Given the greater number of white women in the academy it is more likely that they can look vertically and horizontally within the organization to find someone like themselves, someone who shares their experiences and worldview. This flexibility offers opportunities to seek out others who might help further a career.

> Black women [by contrast] feel their academic opportunities are limited, that there are barriers to their futures in higher education and a built-in isolation in an academic career. Unlike white women and Black men who more frequently are selected for apprenticeships or assistant ships to make 'people developers', Black women have had very few models or champions to encourage and assist them in their development. Black women have had to develop themselves on their own, with no help from whites or Black men, in order to 'make it' in academic institutions. (Carroll, 1982, p. 119)

The importance of having someone to act as professional mentor was spelled out by Beveley Guy-Sheftall (1993), who documented the development of black women's studies at Spelman College (the oldest black women's college in the world). Now Director of a women's centre at Spelman, she pointed to her meeting with Patricia Bell Scott as one of the most momentous occasions in her career.

> Pat and I later became close friends and have worked together, always harmoniously, on several projects within the past few years. . . . It occurs to me that my work at Spelman would not have taken the direction it did were it not for my association with Pat who provided constant guidance. (Guy-Sheftall, 1993, p. 83)

By way of contrast the three black women on my university site are the trail blazers. There are no scripts, and no one sits in the wings prompting us on. Much of what we do is ad-lib. We are creating theory and practice as we go along. This differs from the position of white women lecturers, who not only have opportunities for career development they also follow in the footsteps of other white women who precede them. Furthermore there is the possibility of avoiding competition between themselves and a friend. This is because it is technically possible for white women to make friendships with other white women outside of their academic subject area. These option do not really exist for black women primarily because there are so very few black women at any level within the organization to make friends with.

Developing a career might mean being in competition with the only other black woman in the school, on the site or even, in some cases, within the university. Opening up opportunities for friendships and career options for black women must therefore include increasing the number of black women in the academy. It also means that white women must address the ways in which their behaviour contributes to marginalizing black women. Myers for instance argues that white society (including feminists) must first reflect upon their vision for society and recognize that whilst they might advocate cultural pluralism, they often really mean assimilation.

> ... the nonacceptance of 'true' cultural difference is totally outside of the awareness of the dominant cultural group (non-conscious). On a conscious level members of the dominant group are likely not to really know what the 'other' culture is like except on a superficial level (ie, based on the perception and understanding their own culture's conceptual system allows). (Myers, 1980, p. 18)

I suggest that a number of white women feminists assemble together by virtue of a common culture influenced by a particular notion of feminism. Thus sometimes, when they talk and laugh about the books they have read and enjoyed, discuss significant events in feminist theatre and literature, I often find it difficult to find a place where I can even begin to make myself known. Their common heritage is not mine. The history and relationship between their people and my people is one of conquest and exploitation.

Despite my discomfort, I do still strongly believe in the valuing and celebration of difference enough to feel that it is their right to share the positive things and the responsibilities which makes them who they are. I am not as yet convinced, however, that the consequences of this must always be a sense of exclusion on my part. I believe that white women need to recognize and acknowledge their culture (hooks, 1982; Frankenberg, 1993). Until this is recognized, and they are made aware of their identities, they will continue to have problems with variation. Hence appreciation of 'race' is a prerequisite to moving towards alliance and an understanding that women can be both oppressed and oppressors. We are social beings and thus move in and out of these roles throughout the day. We are soaked in ideologies of inequality and the relative worth of human beings, thus we act oppressively towards others, and correspondingly 'cope' with others' oppression of us. Yet because a number of white women academics fear the visibility of the process by which they swing from being victims towards being oppressors, they are unwilling to recognize the power of their common heritage. Thus they so easily support one another when certain critical issues are concerned. For instance, I continue to be amazed at the speed with which certain white women are able to support one another in their racism, whilst arguing that the issue under consideration does not involve 'race' at all.

Marginalizing black women in the academy and expecting them to fit unproblematically into the existing Eurocentric system tends to be the norm. Where there is conflict black women are likely to be the disadvantaged participants. Compared with black women white women in the academy have greater access to power in order to punish. Part of this involves the greater access they have to positions of authority, as well as a shared culture with powerful people, that is white men. Eurocentricism gives primacy to the values and issues of the white community. I have for instance been told by a white feminist that it is my responsibility to find a mechanism to identify her's and other white people's racism. Unfortunately this approach is far from rare, (Combahee River Collective, 1977), and places emphasis on the oppressed to help provide the solution to the problems of their persecutors.

> As white women, we continually expect women of color to bring us to an understanding of our racism. White women rarely meet to examine collectively our attitudes, our actions, and most importantly, our resistance to change. (Pence, 1982, p. 46)

Again, it was suggested that I work on this matter in a manner which the organization found palatable. Further, it was made absolutely clear that complaints of racism were deemed both disloyal and ungrateful, given the 'support' already dispensed to me. This tendency to respond to wider problems with an individualized approach, characterizes western society and is a source of potential conflict between black and white women.

Cultural differences may become most apparent in times of swingeing academic cut backs, as it is during these times that the climate for worker exploitation increases. Given the differences in cultural expectations and approaches to work, this can leave black women in a marginalized position. Whilst white women may resent the nature of their exploitation by both capital and men, they often respond to that exploitation in ways which white men find relatively comfortable. In general western white women pull from a pool of stoicism which has a history based in the Protestant work ethic. A fair day's work for a fair day's pay, 'just get on with things and don't complain'. For black women generally, and African-Caribbean women specifically, with a history of labour exploitation which includes colonialism and slavery, to make the best of things without protest, is to make invisible the problems which are part of the abuse. This behaviour is seldom seen within a political context and contributes to the further marginalization of black women.

Surviving and thriving within higher education is fraught with dangers for black women because of the extent of their disadvantage within it. Links with other black women within and external to the organization are, I would argue, an essential part of good mental health.

I have developed friendships with black (Asian and African) women colleagues in this and other professions. I have also looked 'down-wards' within the university. For example, I count as a friend an African woman research student and two word-processor operators who have subsequently moved on. Although black women students are a potential source of friends, I avoid friendship at that level, because I believe this to be too difficult a relationship to manage, given the difference in power relations. I have always argued the need to provide everyone with the same opportunity to evaluate my teaching. Similarly, I wish to safeguard my professional integrity as a just assessor of academic and practical work within an environment uncomplicated by the factor of friendship. Once students have completed their course, the situation changes and I have been able to take up the opportunity to develop a social relationship.

I believe that the strength of these combined relationships with black women inside and outside of the university are the strong foundation on which it has been possible to begin taking risks with women across the colour divide.

Friendships across the Divide: Black and White Women in Academia

The extent of gendered-racism and racialized-sexism which black women face within the academy, alongside the responses of many white feminists to that oppression, certainly calls into question whether it is possible to make trusting and sustained friendships with white women in higher education. Despite this, my own belief is that

> [t]here absolutely has to be some sort of bridge between black and white feminists whether it happens as a movement, an organisation or as individuals. (Lena, 1986, p. 21)

However, as Lorde (1979) has stated, this can never be on the basis of those who currently have the most power. Neither can we bond simply on the basis of shared victimization, or in response to a false sense of a common enemy. This is too frail a foundation on which to build a mass social movement. Similarly, we cannot join together 'on the terms set by the dominant ideology of the culture' (hooks, 1984, p. 47). This is because dominant ideologies give primacy to the needs of more the powerful women amongst us. It is at this point that I think it would be useful to analyse what it is about the few white women friends I have which draws us together.

What characterizes my friendships with chosen white women is their distance from the centre. My white feminist friends are marginalized women, whether it has been imposed from the outside or by themselves. They already start with a lived understanding of difference, which whilst it may not be the same as my own, means that their outsider status has a rawness which binds us together. I would not argue that we are necessarily in the same boat, but that we know that we need each other because we are in danger of being submerged by others more powerful than ourselves.

We have no choice but to take chances in order to survive, and it is this taking of risks, sometimes on one another's behalf, which builds trust and which marks out friendships. These actions speak louder than any words. Thus these women have a similar relationship with organizations, that is they have a healthy irreverence which allows them to unravel the ways in which they and others are being exploited and oppressed. They, like myself, have shown a willingness to take risks which are based on a structural analysis, and thus have been empathic to the daily humiliations which include gendered-racism and racialized-sexism. My friends do not fear black women because of their difference, and have made efforts to understand and celebrate them.

References

BAILEY, D., HAYNES, M., MCGREGOR, V. and SARAGA, E. (1996) *Equal Opportunities, Open Teaching Toolkit*, Milton Keynes: Open University.

BELL SCOTT, P. (1982) 'Debunking sapphire: Towards a non-racist and non-sexist social science', in HULL, G.T., BELL SCOTT, P. and SMITH, B. (eds) *All the Women Are White All the Blacks Are Men but Some of Us Are Brave: Black Women's Studies*, New York: The Feminist Press, pp. 85–92.

BRYAN, B., DADZIE, S. and SCAFE, S. (1985) *The Heart of the Race: Black Women's Lives in Britain*, London: Virago Press.

CARROLL, C.M. (1982) 'Three's a crowd: The dilemma of the black woman in higher education,' in HULL, G.T., BELL SCOTT, P. and SMITH, B. (eds) *All the Women Are White, All the Blacks Are Men, but Some of Us Are Brave*: Black Women's Studies, New York: The Feminist Press, pp. 115–28.

COMBAHEE RIVER COLLECTIVE (1977) 'A black feminist statement', in HULL, G.T., BELL SCOTT, P. and SMITH, B. (eds) *All the Women Are White, All the Blacks Are Men, but Some of Us Are Brave*: Black Women's Studies, New York: The Feminist Press, pp. 13–22.

DEAL, T.E. and KENNEDY, A.A. (1983) 'Culture: A new look through old lenses', *Journal of Applied Behavioural Science*, November, p. 501.

EQUAL OPPORTUNITIES AND RACE RELATIONS DEPARTMENT (1994) *The Ethnic Minority Population of Derbyshire: A Statistical Study from the 1991 Census of Population*, Derby, Derbyshire County Council Offices.

ESSED, P. (1991) *Understanding Everyday Racism: An Interdisciplinary Theory*, London: Sage.

FRANKENBERG, R. (1993) *White Women Race Matters: The Social Construction of Whiteness*, London: Routledge.

FULANI, L. (ed.) (1988) *The Psychopathology of Everyday Racism and Sexism*, New York and London: Harrington Park Press.

FRENCH, W.L. and BELL, C.H. JNR. (1990) *Organisation Development: Behavioral Science Interventions for Organisation Improvement*, 4 edition, Engelwood Cliffs, New Jersey: Prentice-Hall.

GUY-SHEFTALL, B. (1993) 'A black feminist perspective on transforming the academy: The case of Spelman College', in: JAMES, S. and BUSIA, A.P.A. (eds) *Theorizing Black Feminisms, the Visionary Pragmatism of Black Women*, London: Routledge, pp. 77–89.

HEARN, J. and PARKIN, W. (1987) *Sex at Work: The Power and Paradox of Organisation Sexuality*. Brighton: Wheatsheaf.

HINE, D.C., KING, W. and READ, L. (eds) (1995) *We Specialize in the Wholly Impossible: A Reader in Black Women's History*, Brooklyn, New York: Carlson Publishing.

HOOKS, B. (1982) *Ain't I a Woman, Black Women and Feminism*, London: Pluto Press.

HOOKS, B. (1984) *Feminist Theory from Margin to Center*, Boston: South End press.

HULL, G.T., BELL SCOTT, P. and SMITH, B. (eds) (1982) *All the Women Are White, All the Blacks Are Men, but Some of Us Are Brave*: Black Women's Studies, New York: The Feminist Press.

JAMES, S. and BUSIA, A.P.A. (eds) (1993) *Theorizing Black Feminisms, the Visionary Pragmatism of Black Women*, London: Routledge.

JEWELL, K.S. (1993) *From Mammy to Miss America and Beyond: Cultural Images and the Shaping of US Social Policy*, London: Routledge.

LEBSOCK, S. (1984) *The Free Women of Petersberg*, New York: W.W. Norton and Company.

LORDE, A. (1979) 'The master's tools will never dismantle the master's house: Comments at the personal and the political panel', Second sex conference, New York, 29 September.

LORDE, A. (1984) *Sister Outsider: Essays and Speeches by Audre Lorde*, CA: The Crossing Press Feminist series.

McKAY, N.Y. (1993) 'Acknowledging differences: Can women find unity through diversity?', in JAMES, S. and BUSIA, A.P.A. (eds) *Theorizing Black Feminisms, the Visionary Pragmatism of Black Women*, London: Routledge, pp. 267–82.

MIRZA, H.S. (1994) 'Black women in higher education: Defining a space/finding a space', in MORLEY, L. and WATSON, V. (eds) *Critical Agents for Change*, pp. 145–55.

MORRISON, T. (1979) 'Cinderella's stepsisters', Address to a Barnard college audience, May 1979.

MYERS, L.W. (1980) *Black Women: Do They Cope Better?*, Englewood Cliffs, New Jersey: Prentice-Hall.

OMOLADE, B. (1994) *The Rising Song of African American Women*, New York and London: Routledge.

PAT (1986) 'Apart or a part?', *Spare Rib*, pp. 44–5.

PENCE, E. (1982) 'Racism — A white issue', in HULL, G.T., BELL SCOTT, P. and SMITH, B. (eds) *All the Women Are White, All the Blacks Are Men, but Some of Us Are Brave*: Black Women's Studies, New York: The Feminist Press, pp. 45–7.

SELZNICK, P. (1957) *Leadership in Administration*, Evaston, Ill: Peterson Row.

SMITH, B. (ed.) (1983) *Home Girls: A Black Feminist Anthology*, New York: Kitchen Table: Women of Color Press.

UNKNOWN (1986) 'Can black and white women work together?', *Spare Rib*, July, pp. 18–21.

WILSON, A. (1978) *Finding a Voice: Asian Women in Britain*, London: Virago.

12   Uneven Developments — Women's Studies in Higher Education in the 1990s

Gabriele Griffin

Introduction

We have all been guilty of it — triumphalist narratives of the inexorable advance of women's studies in the academy. The opening of Diane Richardson and Victoria Robinson's (1993) *Introducing Women's Studies* is just one such — very typical — example.

> Over the past two decades women's studies has become established as an important field of study in many countries across the world. It is now a rapidly expanding area both in terms of the number of courses and in the proliferation of feminist theories from a variety of perspectives. (1993, p. xvii)

These triumphalist narratives have served us — and by 'us' I mean women working in women's studies — well, both psychologically in terms of helping to decrease our sense of marginalization, and strategically within education: on their backs we have argued for the establishment of women's studies courses and for the creation of women's studies posts.

I do not wish to challenge the validity of these narratives. It is the case that women's studies in the UK has grown rapidly over the past few years as regards numbers of courses, students, teachers and textbooks (Brown et al., 1993; Grace, 1991; Griffin et al., 1994, p. 2). But it has grown against a grain of a backlash against feminism (Faludi, 1991; French, 1992), in a context of continuing fragmentation among diverse feminist groups (Griffin, 1995) and in a climate where many women, particularly younger women, are not as a matter of course attracted to feminism (Morgan, 1995). One could argue therefore that this is, in fact, a considerable achievement and so it is.

In the last year or two, however, I have begun to feel increasingly uneasy about our stories of the progressive advance about women's studies, and for the following reasons. At least a dozen women I know who teach women's studies have had opportunities within the last two years of moving into women's studies full-time, or of applying for women's studies posts, or of changing their job title to one which contains women's studies, i.e. 'Lecturer in women's studies', 'Professor of women's studies' etc. Very few women have done so. There are now only five professors of women's studies — with that being their explicit title — in the UK

(Mary Evans — U of Kent, Jalna Hanmer — Bradford U, Gabriele Griffin — Leeds Metropolitan U, Maggie Humm — U of East London, Sue Lees — U of North London). The reasons offered for not moving into women's studies full-time or, indeed, moving out of the subject in terms of location within an institution tend to centre on a fear of being marginalized by working in an area which — after all — is not as well established as other disciplines and the longevity of which within higher education seems unpredictable, coupled with the frustrations inherent in such a situation some of which I shall discuss below.

With the exception of the Roehampton Institute of Higher Education, there are still no women's studies departments in this country even though research centres such as the ones at the Universities of Lancaster, York and Warwick, for instance, exist in many institutions. Many women's studies staff therefore continue to be based in disciplines other than women's studies and commonly combine working in a 'traditional' discipline like English or sociology with some work in women's studies, and, when in doubt, the 'home' discipline becomes the port of retreat or of attribution. This has knock-on effects in terms such as the Research Assessment Exercise. It also affects women's career prospects within women's studies for it means that there are relatively few full-time women's studies posts compared to the numbers of women actually teaching women's studies. This in turn acts as a disincentive to commit oneself wholly to women's studies as being identified with a full-time women's studies post can both fetter the individual to the institution (there not being many other similar jobs elsewhere advertised) and it creates a career impasse in that there are few more senior posts in the subject to move to. To suggest that one look abroad and choose a kind of voluntary academic exile is no answer to this issue — even if there are more women's studies posts in the USA than in the UK, for example. Apart from the fact that such a move is not an easy thing to do either from a personal perspective or in terms of the competition from other academics worldwide, it also does nothing to promote women's studies in the UK which is what must concern all women in women's studies here at the moment. It is interesting to note in this context that a recent volume about influential women thinkers indicates that even women who have been very influential in women's studies such as bell hooks and Carol Gilligan, to name two American women professors, are not professors of women's studies but of English and education respectively (Griffiths, 1996).

To date, the chairs in women's studies in the UK, for example, have all been personal chairs — they are specific to the women who have them. This means that not only are there no chairs in women's studies advertised for women to move to but also that there is no mobility beyond a certain point — it is very difficult to move to or from a women's studies post. Additionally, when a woman who has a women's studies chair goes to another job, there is no onus on the institution she leaves to replace her either at all or with someone at professorial level. Generally, many more jobs are advertised in other, more traditional disciplines than in women's studies which makes establishing yourself or remaining in a discipline other than women's studies a much more attractive prospect than becoming a 'women's studies person'.

In my own case, my move from one institution to another gave the institution I left the opportunity of appointing someone of more junior rank than myself so that the chair in women's studies at that institution was effectively lost. My professorship in women's studies at Leeds Metropolitan University means that there is one new personal chair in the field but the overall numbers have not changed. This helps to create a glass ceiling which contributes to the indirect policing of women's studies as a subject (Davidson and Cooper, 1992, p. 17). The fewer senior posts there are in a subject the less likely that subject is to be represented in the committees and meetings where higher education policy decisions are made. The death of 'small' departments in areas such as Russian, music and philosophy which were closed as a result of the higher education funding cuts in the early 1980s should provide food for thought here.

When I decided that I wanted to move to a new institution while maintaining my base in women's studies, I had to take a job which is predominantly managerial and where the professorship in women's studies is effectively secondary to my role as head of school. The alternative was to move sideways or downgrade, neither of which I particularly wanted to do. In my first appraisal in my current job — in this day and age I am sure most of us are the objects or subjects of such a process (see Thomas in this volume) — the issue of my role and work in women's studies did not figure at all. I am tempted to argue that the institution I moved to indulged my 'whim' for women's studies (that is, appointed me to a professorship in women's studies) because they were actually more interested in other aspects of my professional self. But then the job advertised was that of a head of school, with the professorship being an 'optional extra', for the postholder if she fitted appropriate criteria.

Mary Evans, Professor of women's studies at Kent University, has highlighted (1995, p. 77) the shift in academe from a culture which was patriarchal to one where the academy is no longer male in the simple, chauvinistic sense of the period 1945 to the mid-1970s, it is now an institution of managerial masculinity, rather than masculinity *per se*. This new managerialism has led to the creation and/or renaming of posts in academe which bear titles familiar from industry such as chief executive etc. The question of the extent to which women do and/or should participate in this managerialist culture is one that poses dilemmas for feminists, particularly when writing on women in management (Morley and Walsh, 1995; Davidson and Cooper, 1992) frequently and unquestioningly reproduces the gendered binarisms which much recent feminist theory (Butler, 1993; Butler, 1990; Moore, 1994; Phelan, 1993; Walby, 1990) has sought to question. The underlying assumption often is that women who have what might be described as a career or who achieve senior positions thereby either forsake their feminist domain and/or align themselves with men (Griffiths, 1996, pp. 2–5). This view can act as a very effective deterrent for women in applying for senior positions. But not to participate in the hierarchical world of academe beyond a certain level serves to reinforce all the clichés about women's limited ability, about glass ceilings, about horizontal sex segregation in the job market which it must be in women's interest to explode (Davidson and Cooper, 1992). This means that women have to deal with the issue of power for to participate in hierarchical structures also means to engage in positions of differential power. One of the most constructive debates about women and power has taken place among Italian feminists who not only recognize that diverse women have different degrees of power (Milan Women's Bookstore Collective, 1990; Bono and Kemp, 1991) but who also advocate the deliberate use of such power for the empowerment of women. As Gayatri Spivak (1993) and bell hooks (1994) have demonstrated, without participation there is little possibility for producing the kinds of changes in knowledge and institutional structures feminists have promoted so avidly (Alcoff and Potter, 1993; Barrett and Phillips, 1992; Code, 1991).

Women's studies is still not recognized as a separate category for the purposes of research assessments and other formal, funding-related exercises. Being subsumed under 'sociology' — as it was in the 1996 Research Assessment Exercise — which does not do justice to the diversity of women's studies invisibilizes the subject. In the autumn of 1995 the Women's Studies Network UK conducted a survey of women's studies tutors and whether or not they would make a strategic case in their own institutions for being put into a separate grouping for the 1996 Research Assessment Exercise. A letter to this effect was sent out to all higher education institutions in the UK which have women's studies in their programs. Celia Davies, who coordinated the responses received 12 in all (including her own) — a disappointingly small number. Of these 'only one . . . looked as if it just might at that point try to submit as women's studies' (Davies, 1996). It became clear that few, if any, women's studies groups of staff would put together a case for women's studies as a category in its own right. As Celia Davies wrote: 'The response was frequently that women's studies was taught but not researched collectively, that groups were dispersed and not strong enough to take this route' (Davies, 1996). The pattern is that institutions have traditions of deciding above individuals' heads into what research unit they put staff so as to maximize returns; these decisions are frequently based on history, i.e. on past performance, itself determined by the longer established disciplines from which previous research groupings have emerged. Institutions — and individuals — are unwilling to take the risk of arguing for women's studies, thereby potentially 'weakening' the entries they make to disciplines the previous ratings for which they know. Thus if a unit of assessment, say sociology, in a given institution achieved a high rating in the 1992 Research Assessment Exercise, institutional expectation, usually directly expressed, is that the members of this unit do at least as well if not better in the 1996 exercise. Many women seem to feel unable even to make the case for a women's studies category in their institution in whatever context (Brown Packer, 1995; Davies and Holloway, 1995; Bannerji et al., 1991). This is indicative of a number of issues: women's perception of their own powerlessness to intervene in institutional decisions; women's perception of the vulnerability of women's studies which they do not want to augment by challenging institutional decisions; women's ambivalence about being associated with a non-traditional and contentious discipline; women's loyalty to subject areas with which they have been closely aligned during their working lives; insecurity concerning the outcome of a women's studies submission as opposed to one to a discipline which has already been through the assessment cycle; etc.

Anecdotal evidence suggests that recruitment on many women's studies courses both at undergraduate and at postgraduate level over the last two years or so has been down or just about kept to the level it was previously (the concern about this development is such that the Women's Studies Network UK Association is now — spring 1997 — supporting research supervised by Diana Leonard at the Institute of Education, London, to investigate the extent of this phenomenon). When I presented this chapter as a paper at the Women in Higher Education Conference at Preston (March, 1996) one woman from London declared that their numbers of students were up from previous years. However, my own involvement with courses in two institutions where I have taught women's studies, and on five courses where I am or was external examiner as well as many talks with women's studies colleagues elsewhere lead me to the conclusion that overall recruitment is even or down rather than up. The women I have talked to often relate this to the backlash against feminism, to funding problems (particularly at postgraduate level), and to the precariousness of the discipline itself. The fact that recruitment to higher education in a number of subjects, particularly at part-time level, is declining (Midgley, 1997, p. 19) and that women's studies in this respect suffers no more than other areas is not often acknowledged. Competition in higher education for students has increased while funding for students has become more problematic and at postgraduate level, except for the particularly brilliant and fortunate few, has never been there. Women in women's studies seem to worry very easily that women's studies might be a bubble about to burst and sometimes attribute this to women's studies in itself rather than to other factors affecting higher education as a whole. Not all of the problems women's studies faces are subject-specific but we frequently see them as such. The sense of embattlement around women's studies has clearly not gone away.

Many women's studies courses have experienced difficulties in getting the institutional support — administrative and financial as well as in terms of staffing — necessary to ensure their smooth running (Evans, 1995; Hanmer, 1991; Lees, 1991). Frequently, only one woman, often junior, is in charge of a women's studies course; if she leaves or problems occur because she does not have the institutional clout to get the resources necessary for the course, the institutionally easy way out is to curtail the course or even to abandon it.

Why have all these difficulties arisen? I would suggest that the reasons for the current state of women's studies in the UK are associated with changes in higher education which have affected everyone within the academy but in different ways. Many of the first women's studies courses, particularly at undergraduate level and in the so-called — but actually now not so — 'new' universities, came into institutional being as options or courses within other disciplines and as part of degrees which were not degrees in women's studies. When universities and colleges went modular from the second half of the 1980s (Newbold and Wade, 1995), this seemed ideal as a take-off point for women's studies degrees. At last we could all be together in one vast modular scheme where the home base or original discipline did not seem to matter that much anymore, particularly as there was a simultaneous rise in the establishment of course teams or pathway groupings of staff rather than having discipline-based departments. Few other disciplines or courses, however, embraced the diversity of possibilities of choice open to the students of inter- and multi-disciplinary courses in women's studies. Therein lay also one of the real problems for women's studies, history students, for example, even in a modular scheme, turned out on the whole to prefer the equivalent of 'meat and two veg' or, very obviously history-related modules, rather than 'beef and smarties' or, a module in history and one in engineering, for example, particularly by the time they got to the third year. Course teams for degrees in history or other such traditional disciplines found themselves, increasing bureaucracy and other such nuisances notwithstanding, in a not dissimilar position to what they had been in before, that is working together on courses predominantly taken by students who were doing mainly or entirely history modules. The need to liaise outside a subject specific group of staff and students was correspondingly smaller for these people than it was for women's studies participants who needed to work across subject areas, schools, faculties, the traditional divides among disciplines such as arts, social sciences, 'natural' sciences, management and business etc. Institutions themselves, while dissolving departments or re-framing schools, tended not to abolish the macro units to which they had previously worked: there were still faculties of humanities, arts, social sciences, management and business etc. The overall effect of this was that for the traditional disciplines business in many respects remained business as usual and institutions saw little need to change this.

This had a detrimental effect on women's studies because — being a multi- or inter-disciplinary subject — it could not easily work to the traditional structures maintained at macro level. For instance: with women's studies lecturers in diverse faculties, schools, and disciplines the question of how to request staff hours, especially if the woman who has to do these negotiations has neither bargaining power nor clout intra-institutionally because she is too junior in status, becomes a very difficult one.

Not all courses are hampered by such problems of intra-institutional negotiation. But I have come across at least three — located in both old and new universities — where difficulties of negotiating resources and staffing, a problem due to the mismatch between the institutional macro structures and the dispersal of women's studies staff across a range of schools and faculties, have led to radical revisions of the courses involved, usually downsizing them and considering their abandonment. It is also the case that some institutions take the line that if you teach women's studies you do so in your own time — in other words, it has the status of an academically invisible and unrecognized activity, a kind of leisure pursuit which relies on staff being committed enough to teach the subject even if no recognition in terms of hours provided on the timetable, for instance, is attached to this. This is a crass form of exploitation.

The dispersal of women interested in, and teaching, women's studies issues across a vast range of disciplines raises the question of the feasibility of a women's studies department, with some maintaining that women's studies in any event is not a discipline (Bowles, 1983). I do not want to get into that debate here, save to say that it seems to me that women's studies can have the status of a discipline in academe as much as any other, already established area of enquiry — and for all the arguments to do with coherent bodies of knowledge, specific research methodologies etc. typically made for a discipline as a discipline (Coyner, 1983). More to the point is the question of how women doing women's studies in academe ought to strategize in order to maintain their subject as a viable area. The answer seems to me to be both growth and diversification or specialization. The two go in tandem. Both depend on working towards and achieving a critical mass of staff which, even in this day and age of extreme financial constraints in higher education, can be achieved. It can be done in at least two ways. One of these is to move towards specialization, to have for instance women's studies in law degrees, or women's studies courses that are entirely arts-related or social sciences-related, and where all staff have an academic and research interest in one of these fields. This may be regarded as either retrenchment or specialization; the effect is to align the course more obviously with institutional macro structures and thus have easier access to resources in staffing and in other terms. Two institutions have implemented this already. One of the positive reasons for setting up such more specialized courses, especially at postgraduate level, is that we are now beginning to see the first graduates of women's studies undergraduate courses which are very generalized come through — specialization is one way forward for these women who are seeking to build on the knowledge gained at undergraduate level. Against this one might argue that the inter-disciplinarity of women's studies gets lost in such specialization. This may well be true but we need to ask ourselves:

- to what extent, historically, women's studies courses with very diverse modules came about precisely because there was only one woman in any given discipline in any one institution willing and able to teach women's studies, i.e. to what extent course configurations were driven by necessity rather than (or, as much as) by curricular and other considerations;
- how inter-disciplinary women's studies courses really are.

The women's studies courses — as opposed to modules outside such courses — which I have been involved with have had, with one exception, very particular disciplinary parameters, based on resident staff expertise and generally being either arts or social sciences oriented. The integration of other subject areas such as archaeology, geography, pure sciences, etc. into women's studies courses has, at least in my experience in this country, been very limited indeed. This is not a criticism, merely a recognition that women's studies comes in many guises and exists both as discrete courses and as modules within courses that have other titles. It gives those engaged in women's studies some freedom to think creatively about how to move the subject forward.

An alternative to specialization is to begin to lobby for much larger configurations of women's studies staff than many traditional disciplines in the UK usually have, i.e. looking at something like schools of women's studies with 40 or more staff so that both generalist and specialist courses can be offered from within one unit which is well embedded into general institutional structures and thus has resourcing comparable to that of other schools or large departments. In the UK there is no history of 'thinking big' in this way but critical mass is essential for the survival of any course.

One of the current, but not that recently started, debates in women's studies is its relationship to gender studies (Polity Press, 1994, p. 3). Whatever the arguments about men in feminism (Are men there? Are men capable of being there? Should they be there? etc., Jardine and Smith, 1987; Segal, 1990; Rylance, 1992) and 'gender studies equals masculinity studies' (Walter, 1994), we have to ask ourselves to what extent gender studies has not merely come about because of men wishing to get a slice of the action and because of the influence of queer theory, but also because the women in women's studies felt they needed men's support (especially when it came to the question of 'who is there to teach X?') in a situation where they found themselves to be 'the only one' across a range of disciplines dealing with feminist agendas.

The answer to the issues outlined above is not 'fewer' but 'more': more staff either in more circumscribed courses or as part of much larger women's studies schools. And, more women's studies courses, but more diverse ones. Paradoxically, it is in this context that the changes to research funding and the research assessment exercise can be helpful. In the last two years or so, against the grain of the fragmentation introduced by modularization and other changes in higher education, research funding has increasingly favoured research groups, looking for people collaborating across or within institutions rather than for lone individuals beavering away all by themselves. This has given rise to the opportunity for women to collaborate strategically through joint research projects with a view, ultimately, to setting themselves up as a unit within one institution. Only a small number of women have grasped this opportunity to date, and, given all the demands as regards teaching, administration and research on academics today, this is hardly surprising. In the humanities, for instance, where there is a research tradition of individuals working on their own, women can find it quite difficult to contemplate joint research projects which involve bidding for funding and collaboration beyond carving up what needs doing into smaller sections or chapters which are again undertaken alone. However, strategic collaboration is one of the obvious moves by which we can ensure the survival of women's studies into the twenty-first century. It is a medium-term strategy in that it requires the establishment of collaborations over several, say at least two to three, years before it is possible to point to the successes in terms of funding and publications achieved necessary to make a group of women collaborating the kind of unit an institution will support. It can certainly be done within one institution though it requires planning and commitment. But neither of these are new to women's studies staff. It requires the recognition that we must think bigger and in terms of critical mass in order to promote women's studies. It also requires that we think about the market place and keep asking about the ways in which women's studies is valuable to diverse groups of women. I suspect we do not always do that enough.

It is in this context that I was interested to see York University's Centre for Women's Studies advertise three different Masters courses in an edition of *The Guardian* (6 February 1996, p. 38). The move away from generic women's studies courses to differentially focused ones means that different groups of women with diverse educational and professional needs can be addressed. If this is done from within one unit, that is by having all women's studies students co-located, potential growth is possible — of courses, in student and in staff numbers. Such growth is becoming vital and will see us into the twenty-first century.

References

ALCOFF, L. and POTTER, E. (eds) (1993) *Feminist Epistemologies*, London: Routledge.

BANNERJI, H., CARTY, L., DEHLI, K., HEALD, S. and McKENNA, K. (eds) (1991) *Unsettling Relations: The University As a Site of Feminist Struggle*, Boston, MA: South End Press.

BARRETT, M. and PHILLIPS, A. (eds) (1992) *Destabilizing Theory*, Cambridge: Polity Press.

BONO, P. and KEMP, S. (eds) (1991) *Italian Feminist Thought*, Oxford: Basil Blackwell.

BOWLES, G. (1983) 'Is women's studies an academic discipline?', in BOWLES, G. and DUELLI KLEIN, R. (eds) *Theories of Women's Studies*, London: Routledge and Kegan Paul, pp. 32–45.

BROWN, L., COLLINS, H., GREEN, P. and HUMM, M. (eds) (1993) *The International Handbook of Women's Studies*, London: Harvester Wheatsheaf.

BROWN PACKER, B. (1995) 'Irrigating the sacred grove: Stages of gender equity development', in MORLEY, L. and WALSH, V. (eds) *Feminist Academics: Creative Agents for Change*, London: Taylor and Francis, pp. 42–55.

BUTLER, J. (1990) *Gender Trouble*, London: Routledge.

BUTLER, J. (1993) *Bodies that Matter*, London: Routledge.

CODE, L. (1991) *What Can She Know?* Ithaca: Cornell University Press.

COYNER, S. (1983) 'Women's studies as an academic discipline', in BOWLES, G. and DUELLI KLEIN, R. (eds) *Theories of Women's Studies*, London: Routledge and Kegan Paul, pp. 46–71.

DAVIDSON, M.J. and COOPER, C.L. (1992) *Shattering the Glass Ceiling: The Woman Manager*, London: Paul Chapman.

DAVIES, C. (1996) Personal communication.

DAVIES, C. and HOLLOWAY, P. (1995) 'Troubling transformations: Gender regimes and organizational culture in the academy', in MORLEY, L. and WALSH, V. (eds) *Feminist Academics: Creative Agents for Change*, London: Taylor and Francis, pp. 7–21.

EVANS, M. (1995) 'Ivory towers: Life in the mind', in MORLEY, L. and WALSH, V. (eds) *Feminist Academics: Creative Agents for Change*, London: Taylor and Francis, pp. 73–85.

FALUDI, S. (1991) Backlash: *The Undeclared War against Women*, London: Chatto and Windus.

FRENCH, M. (1992) *The War against Women*, London: Hamish Hamilton.

GRACE (1991) *Women's Studies in the European Community*, Brussels: GRIF.

GRIFFIN, G. (ed.) (1995) *Feminist Activism in the 1990s*, London: Taylor and Francis.

GRIFFIN, G., HESTER, M., RAI, S. and ROSENEIL, S. (eds) (1994) *Stirring It: Challenges for Feminism*, London: Taylor and Francis.

GRIFFITHS, S. (ed.) (1996) *Beyond the Glass Ceiling*, Manchester: Manchester University Press.

HANMER, J. (1991) 'On course: Women's studies — A transitional programme', in AARON, J. and WALBY, S. (eds) *Out of the Margins: Women's Studies in the Nineties*, London: Taylor and Francis, pp. 105–14.

HOOKS, B. (1994) *Teaching to Transgress: Education as the Practice of Freedom*, London: Routledge.

JARDINE, A. and SMITH, P. (eds) (1987) *Men in Feminism*, London: Methuen.

LEES, S. (1991) 'Feminist politics and women's studies: Struggle, not incorporation', in AARON, J. and WALBY, S. (eds) *Out of the Margins: Women's Studies in the Nineties*, London: Taylor and Francis, pp. 90–104.

MIDGLEY, S. (1997) 'Return of the old school ties', *The Times Higher Education Supplement*, 14 February, p. 19.

MILAN WOMEN'S BOOKSTORE COLLECTIVE (eds) (1990) *Sexual Difference*, Bloomington: Indiana University Press.

MOORE, H. (1995) *A Passion for Difference*, Cambridge: Polity.

MORGAN, D. (1994) 'Invisible women: Young women and feminism', in GRIFFIN, G. (ed.) *Feminist Activism in the 1990s*, London: Taylor and Francis, pp. 127–36.

MORLEY, L. and WALSH, C. (eds) (1995) *Feminist Academics: Creative Agents for Change*, London: Taylor and Francis.

NEWBOLD, C. and WADE, W. (1995) *Flexibility in Course Provision in Higher Education: Evaluation Report*, Bristol: Higher Education Funding Council for England.

POLITY PRESS (1994) *The Polity Reader in Gender Studies*, Cambridge: Polity Press.

PHELAN, P. (1993) *Unmarked: The Politics of Performance*, London: Routledge.

RICHARDSON, D. and ROBINSON, V. (1993) *Introducing Women's Studies*, London: Macmillan.

RYLANCE, R. (1992) 'Fellow-travelling with feminist criticism', in CAMPBELL, K. (ed.) *Critical Feminism,* Buckingham: Open University Press, pp. 157–81.

SEGAL, L. (1990) *Slow Motion: Changing Masculinities, Changing Men*, London: Virago.

SPIVAK, G.C. (1993) *Outside the Teaching Machine*, London: Routledge.

WALBY, S. (1990) *Theorizing Patriarchy*, Oxford: Basil Blackwell.

WALTER, N. (1994) 'An agenda for gender', *Independent on Sunday* 23 October, p. 25.

13   Coming Clean: On Being Feminist Editors

Danusia Malina and Sian Maslin-Prothero

Introduction

Our joint experience of editing this collection has changed us, as feminists, and as academics. The procedure by which we were chosen as editors; our subsequent inclusion and exclusion of women's work from the WHEN conference; later commissioning work beyond topics covered at the event; and feedback offered to contributors, has meant we have confronted our practice as feminist editors. Alongside this, our relationship as strangers at the outset and friends and collaborators as the process 'closes', has flashed up differences, commonalities and ambiguities in our approach to the task of feminist editorship. The 'we' as editors we present here in the book is false, rendering invisible layers of negotiation, compromise and solidarity.[1] Like Angela Karach and Denise Roach, 'both of us have been aware of, and have tried as best as we can in these circumstances, not to subsume each of our individual identities and thoughts into an undifferentiated WE' (1992, p. 307). In a piece on collaborative writing as students, these authors underscore the dynamics at play whereby feminists are forced to recognize the positive in differences. Throughout the past months then, we have questioned our individual responses to content, process, and our relationship with each other, as well as with contributors to the book. Our engagement with each 'aspect' has involved fluctuating levels of absorption at various points in the process, in line with what we as individuals prioritized, or were forced to foreground by participants in the project.

We have drawn consciously on past experiences of having our own work edited, of previous editorial responsibility and of feminist literature detailing the dilemmas and excitements of being feminist editors. We realized quickly our knowledge of being edited by others brought mixed emotional baggage to the surface. We share positive memories of being edited for inclusion in non-feminist texts, yet, our involvement in feminist publishing projects has, at times, been less comfortable. Indeed, our looking for 'comfort' in the process led us to consider the distinctiveness of feminist editing as opposed to non-feminist endeavours. One of us, Danusia, had never acted as editor of a book before, while Sian continues to be involved as an editor of non-feminist texts, in the main. Our search for inspiration and direction from feminist material on the subject of feminist editorship left us wanting — many writers allude to the difficulties and dilemmas of the process (see for instance diverse sources such as Keith, 1994; Atwood, 1989; Ginsberg and Lennox, 1996; Russ, 1984; Leslie and Sollie, 1994). Such literature nevertheless offers little analysis of, for instance, the nature of women's gatekeeping and of feminists as silencers of other women's voices within the making of public feminist scholarship (Spender and Kramarae, 1993). Obvious exceptions to this are the writings of black women who have systematically challenged the erasure of black female presence in feminist scholarship (examples being Carty, 1991; hooks, 1989; Ngcobo, 1988). Equally, feminists who do not conform to the heterosexual-middle-class-ablebodied-young-western category of generic woman (Kitzinger and Wilkinson, 1993) not only struggle within mainstream publishing circles but also in feminist publishing channels (Raymond, 1993). We say this because as Dale Spender puts it, 'I would like to . . . claim that feminists are completely open-minded, I have to state that many feminist reviewers find unacceptable those articles that do not share their own political beliefs' (1981, p. 195). As Dale Spender also points out, this problem is not peculiar to feminist journals; rather, it appears that it is feminists alone who are willing to recognize (if not analyse) bias and prejudice in pre-publication practice.

Previous documentation of discrimination against and outright dismissal of women scholars' work in the 1970s and 1980s (Spender, 1989) provided a complex picture of pervasive forms of anti-feminism, both within the academy and outside it in the realm of publishing. The important point here is, this groundbreaking work focused on the significance of male control of pre-publication aspects of the construction and distribution of knowledge — that is, men as gatekeepers within 'mainstream' publishing outlets. The need for feminists to 'tackle male dominance of the mainstream. . . . [and] to conceptualise what is mainstream and what is marginal' (Spender, 1981, p. 198) is difficult to imagine for those of us who as feminists have grown accustomed to the existence of publishing space fought for by earlier generations of women. Such hard won battles have ensured wider audiences are reached by a multiplicity of women's voices and have helped to legitimate women's studies as a discipline (Spender and Kramarae, 1993). Despite acknowledgment that there is no uncontaminated space even within feminist publishing itself (Eagleton, 1996), it would seem that an overall 'hesitancy' towards sustained self-critical reflection remains by those who are in positions to determine what gets published and what does not. Yet, these issues provide just a starting point for any consideration of the political dimensions of publishing, for the spirit of feminism demands more than just an 'add-in-and-stir' publication model of inclusion.

Given the continuing success of women's studies publishing ventures, we might be forgiven for assuming that 'all feminists are keen not to reproduce with respect to other women the unequal relationship of central and peripheral, inclusion and exclusion' (Eagleton, 1996, p. 14). However, as anyone who has ever undertaken the demands of editorship and/or experienced restrictive critical boundaries within feminist scholarship knows, the underbelly of the editorial process is fraught with, 'competing hierarchies of thought which reinscribe the politics of domination by designating work as either inferior, superior, or more or less worthy of attention' (hooks, 1994, p. 64). Since the experience of being edited/being an editor underlines that, 'the locus of control is not always after publication' (Roberts, 1981, p. 187) we are surprised that *the processes that lead to* the feminist printed word have yet to be examined critically when, as Dale Spender and Cheris Kramarae argue, 'women's studies has such a commitment to examining its own processes' (1993, p. 17).

In a context within which productivity measured through publications largely determines the precariousness or not of academic careers (Skeggs, 1995), feminist scholars need more than ever to (re)enter into discussions regarding the barriers to feminist publication for all feminist scholars in their fields. In this we are clearly not thinking just about publication outlets or about scholarly form; rather, we are calling for more debate around the feminist editorial process itself. It seems surprising to us that while long-running debates in feminism over methodological concerns continue, closely guarded secrets remain about the construction of the 'ultimate' knowledge commodity — the polished and neatly presented published book. To echo Skeggs' question here, we too wonder how 'we [can] make evaluations of knowledge we receive if we do not understand how it was produced?' (1995, p. 2).

We think there are lessons to be learned from our experience that may be valuable for other feminist scholars — we invite new insights into the power within and potentials of feminist editing. To this end, our chapter is blatantly personal, attempting to help the reader consider her own experience and possibilities in the realm of feminist editing. We have considered throughout this editorial experience the ways in which we may or may not have utilized a feminist ethics of editorship. We have struggled to define what the delineation of these principles might be for us. We knew we were uncomfortable with the dominant ethos of liberal competitive individualism which perpetuates elitism, hierarchy, objectification and fragmentation of knowledge and of self (Karach and Roach, 1992) — yet we know our approach to responsibilities, especially towards our contributors, has not always matched our 'intentions'.

Looking Back

In what follows we present emergent concerns about our practice as feminist editors via snapshots of dialogues we taped and and later transcribed. By choosing a dialogue style we hope to create a 'talking chapter' which has the potential to capture our critical exchanges, in terms of the differences between us and our points of agreement. Like bell hooks (1994), we are certain writing in dialogue affords us the chance to retain an intimacy and familiarity of expression which an essay format might make less possible. While communicating in this way enables us to retain the uniqueness of our voices; this does not mean that this form is without disadvantage. It has been suggested that a personalized dialogue format is not succinct, is contrived and does not even demonstrate efficiently analysis and synthesis of ideas (Godsell and Miers, 1994). Furthermore, it is possible for dialogues to be critiqued for being non-scholarly or not scholarly enough. Carey Kaplan and Cronan Rose (1993) have most recently been joined by Pamela Cotterill and Gayle Letherby who support this, arguing that feminist collaborative work and/ or work which includes reference to the personal is low down in the academic publications hierarchy (Kaplan and Rose, 1993; Cotterill and Letherby, 1997).

Our intention in writing this piece centres on the notion that in offering access to our conversations we may not only shed light on general processes involved in our editorial work but that, more importantly, we make obvious that what we saw as important in the project was a product of the positioning of ourselves and others we have worked with in the book. Our conversations revealed our shared locations as two white, heterosexual, middle-class, academics in our 30s with children and our different institutional locations as one academic on probation in a 'Russell Group' institution, the other on a permanent contract in a "low status" university, each navigating our way through the dominant paradigms of different disciplines: Danusia in the masculinist, status driven business arena and Sian in the feminised query academic space of nursing studies. Since 'our experiences and understandings of who we (and others) are are always known and interpreted through the discourses and representations available to us' (Skeggs, 1995), we must know how such interpretations are produced. Our locations influenced and informed what we thought, did, how we did what we did and where we looked to as editors.

Feminist Editors in Conversation

DM: One of the ways that this book has made me think about the editorial process is that as a feminist academic I want to view myself as caring. I know this is sick-making stuff but the fantasy that I seem to live with is that feminists will be generous spirited, almost self-sacrificing, especially in relation to other women. I did say this was a fantasy and I know my own shifting feelings of vulnerability in my writing, teaching, and my perceived success *vis à vis* other women affects my ability to be this feminist myself at different times and in various ways.

SM-P: I know what you're talking about — I want to see myself in this way too. I'm concerned about students, teaching, colleagues, the future of higher education (student loans, redundancies, funding cuts etc). We all have our principles (in theory), that is, until we feel threatened and insecure. For example, when our short term contract is up for renewal, or 'downsizing' of the organization follows the latest research assessment exercise (RAE) results. Suddenly we become intensely competitive, altruism goes out of the window; we compete with each other to keep our jobs/positions. Outwardly we still appear to be concerned for each other; behind closed doors we can become defensive and underhand.

DM: What is difficult here is that I'm questioning whether friendships between women in the academy can survive under these conditions. Or are we as feminist academics only interested in protecting our own positions? I realize this paints a black picture but sometimes it feels this way. It's Mary Eagleton who says she cannot easily accommodate the fact that her 'personal trajectory as feminist, white professional, member of an academic institution, is predicated in whatever measure on the absence of other feminists'. She acknowledges, with discomfort, that the fact that inclusivity is a mere fantasy does not make her privilege any more acceptable to her.

SM-P: Yet, with women friends we need not explain everything, there can often be an understanding between feminists based on the fact that we are pitted against one another in patriarchal institutions.

DM: I see what you're getting at but let's think about how we were set up in competition with one another and other feminists to 'secure' this collection as editors. Prior to being 'chosen' to edit the collection we had met twice, I think; once at a functional meeting to organize the 1996 WHEN conference and then again at the event itself. When the publishers looked to appoint editors the commit-tee was asked if they would like to put forward cvs. We knew nothing about each other (hardly), we had not even spoken out of group discussion, did not attend the same conference sessions but did submit exposures of our academic selves. We still do not know, to this day, why we were chosen, what criteria were used for selec-tion, what our cvs suggested that made us 'suitable enough' candidates. Isn't this surprising in a feminist-driven project? I wonder how those who submitted along-side us discovered they were not chosen?

SM-P: But our relationship has moved from strangers to trusted friends. We chose deliberately to get to know each other as women. We spent time, often we could ill afford, to explore our shared experiences. We found we'd both been non-traditional students when we had already been mothers for some time; we found we'd lived in the same places, even during over-lapping times but not knowing each other at the time; how our upbringing held similar messages about femininity; and our views on men, marriage and heterosexuality produced laughter and recog-nition of struggles. There has been a lot of humour — sometimes irreverent. From this an honesty between us developed so that we could explore the differences between us also. Remember when we talked about the different ways we go about our academic careers — you seemed more focused, strategic and instrumental and I seemed to say I was looking for the easiest routes — daring, if you like in small chunks. This has impacted on the way we have gone about the editing — you challenged the content and process and at times this has been yet more burdens on an already crowded work schedule.

DM: I agree we've arrived at a place of compromise here by building on our commonalities. I think this has been pretty easy considering our shared locations as white, middleclass and so on. But I think our investment has also been about our career building too. I knew we'd be up for scrutiny as academics, as feminists at stages in our career when we can't afford derision — can you ever? — the aca-demic community is not exactly a safe place. Safer for some than others, of course. On the one hand, I was honoured to become an editor with you, on the other I was petrified. This was about working on a feminist text, which brought back memories of being a mediocre women's studies student at Lancaster taught by just the fem-inists who might now read the book; and the other issue was about working with a feminist whose feminism might be worlds apart from my own.

SM-P: Yes, that's interesting because we were not asked to provide any indication of our feminist stance(s) — was it assumed we would somehow meld our views or not, or was it assumed we would push these away in our editing of other feminists' work? None of this is clear, even now. And if we look back to the way we chose the papers, it was clear we picked those papers we felt were topical, of quality, those which ideally integrated theory and experience and the ones we felt did not suggest feminism is univocal. These weren't the only issues though, were they? We considered where academics were located, in terms of the academic hierarchy so the text had some 'weighty feminists' in it — so much for our wish to work against hierarchy! — plus we agreed we wanted a balanced book which gave opportunity to those already published as well as to those women at earlier stages in their careers.

DM: The problem is that it feels as if we were always imagining attacks on our scholarly credentials from non-feminists and feminists, especially as white heterosexuals. This is just what Nadya Aisenberg and Mona Harrington (1988) call the practice of self-censorship where feminists modify content and form in order to gain acceptance and of course to pacify those against them. It felt like constantly covering my back. These imaginary enemies have followed us throughout the process, don't you think?

SM-P: Well, yes, but I think of this in terms of specific moments in the project when these 'enemies' have loomed large. For instance, when we compared our choice of papers, we found few differences — other than you seemed to have a more critical stance towards the work. Once we decided on the final compilation, we realized there were glaring gaps. It was at this stage, we became nervous and had long discussions about tokenism in filling these so-called 'gaps' — for example with contributions from black women, lesbians, disabled feminists, women addressing class issues and so forth. We were hampered by the fact that some contributors we'd chosen did not necessarily make their locations clear. This brought us up against queries about the criteria we used to select work. Was it that our ethnocentric, hetero views had blinded us to papers which challenged us? Was it quality concerns that led us to reject such work? In fact, we wondered if we had deliberately chosen papers which matched our views.

DM: So, we trawled over the work again deliberating on just those questions. The selection shifted a little, but it did not alter radically. And then we sought out work by women on disability and black feminist experience in academe, with voices on our shoulders whispering tokenism, tokenism. The thing is, there is strong pressure on editors to include representations of race, class, sexuality and disability within work and what I'm not saying is that this is unreasonable. It's that this is not always possible — laying editors, no-one else, open to critique. Both the rejection of the original work and the subsequent inclusion of women's work not presented at the conference raised futher problems, if you remember. One rejected author wanted explanations about our reasons for not accepting her work. As she said at the time, not another book about women in higher education which focuses only on academics. Her challenge we met with a letter telling her this was not so and giving, I recall, rather superficial reasons for not including her work. What more could we have said? On top of this there were questions from existing contributors about our ethics in commissioning work from women beyond the WHEN network. This one's difficult because our ethics were pulled in at least two directions. Yes, this book comes from the conference but what happens when the papers do not 'fit' the framework we as editors had imposed on the book, and where the papers do not cover issues we, again, considered important. I guess what I'm saying is, who has control of this process and in whose interests were we working? Contributors, ourselves, other women?

SM-P: Which brings us to the point of thinking about editors as developers. Certainly, the process develops us — we need publications on our cv. We want the experience of editing such a collection, not only for task related development, but also as a networking process. Networking, exposure to other feminist work and meeting with feminist researchers is endangered within institutional climates where funding for conferences is being cut — so this work develops our knowledge of work and of feminist authors. The development process is bound up in mutual reciprocity though — in turn contributors also want, even need, their work published for the very same reasons as us, such as the next RAE. But the networking possibilities, at least in the way we have managed the project, have been limited. We sent a synopsis of chapters to each author showing who was participating with the key arguments of each chapter but that was all. Some authors happen to work in the same universities, others have worked previously together, but our knowledge of connections between authors as a result of this book is nil.

DM: Of course, what we haven't mentioned is that not all feminists think about publications in such an instrumental fashion — dissemination of feminist research is not just a means to an end, a publication achieved, it is bound up in feminist hopes for transforming academic disciplines. However, I still think it's significant that we talked about the impact of our editorial relationship with authors and future contact with them as feminist academics. In other words, we were treading a fine line between offering critique, for instance about levels of analysis in chapters, or balance between theoretical debate and experience, while hoping to retain the 'good humour' of each contributor. This presented difficulties where authors didn't submit on time, or occasions when our critique was met by silence and text remained unchanged. When we offered feedback, we wanted to enter into negotiations but tensions arose where we felt obliged to point out ambiguities and inconsistencies, as we saw them.

SM-P: How we dealt with issues like the ones you mention depended on the level of relationship built with each contributor. The fact that we divided the authors between us meant we developed stronger communication with some than others. The crux of the issue for me is that receipt of feedback about chapters is not handled evenly — suggestions are easier to take from some people than others. I would also say that feedback is more difficult to give to some individuals than others also. What I'm talking about here is power differentials between feminists. As a relative newcomer to the academy, I have found it problematic to (comfortably) critique the work of feminists not long ago I was citing as a student. Perhaps getting feedback from less established feminists like us is likewise harder to swallow than from individuals who have track records in the field. This raises the idea that development from editor to contributor and contributor to editor is bound up in positionality also.

DM: Absolutely. My experience of this from a different perspective has come from having to face up to my false ideas about disability. Although you had responsibility for Sally and therefore I had less contact with her at the individual level. It was not until reading her chapter in draft form that I confronted the assumptions I held about her particular disability. I felt ashamed that I'd imagined her as a wheelchair user. I couldn't have been more wrong. Exactly what she was writing about — ignorance, lack of support etc — I had to accept I exhibited it all. Yet, I had searched for a disabled feminist academic to take space in the book. This has been humbling.

SM-P: Being smacked in the face with our own restricted views is necessary, and as Mary Eagleton argues, 'relatively privileged feminists have to hold onto a sense of embarassment and of ethics, not as a self-lacerating indulgence but as a necessary spur to political action' (1996, p. 19). We have to acknowledge that, as in feminist research which aims to be emancipatory rather than exploitative, editing relationships can never be reciprocal because of the power inherent in the position of editor.

DM: So, in practice, the danger to manipulate contributors/contributions is there throughout the process, and it is up to individual editors to discern how 'their feminism' will inform the practice known as feminist editorship. As Letitia Peplau suggests, 'Feminist scholarship is a source of inspiration, not a set of rules' (1994, p. 44). As feminists therefore, we need to think critically not about 'correct' forms of editorship; rather, we need to illuminate and articulate the process by which feminist scholars are building their editing to reflect feminist principles.

Looking Forward

The above dialogue suggests that there are a number of subject positions feminists can take up in relation to themselves and others when engaged in feminist editorship. We have begun to make sense of our experiences by regarding our practice in the following ways. At times we felt akin to occupational guards, especially when we selected and rejected work, when we gave feedback which alters substantive issues, and when we advised about the form that this work 'should' take. We also recognized feminist editorship involves being a developer of others, as well as of ourselves, requiring as it does vigilance and honesty if we are to avoid furthering disadvantage against other feminists. Our role as protectors has emerged when at times we felt we should remind women of their vulnerability. We are thinking here about institutional insecurity where women have laid bare the extent of discrimination in the institutions within which they work. Our dilemmas here meant that we could not let women open themselves to attack, as a result of their printed chapters by those within institutional sites, who believe feminist scholarship is illegitimate. This we regard as editors being occupational safekeepers. The potential for editors as friends extends beyond the relationship between the editors themselves, though this has proved invaluable as a source of support and nourishment — the ensuing friendships with contributors developed within the editorial process has shown us the fruits of collaboration, mindful as we have become of the potential for misabuse of the power of editors in these relationships. Recognition that this power is not fixed, and that it flows between people so that, 'everybody has some of it, some area of choice, of ability to affect things his [sic] way' (Worsley, 1973, p. 250) reminds us that a dialectical balance of power exists between editors and contributors at varying stages of the process. At the last stages of submission of final copy to the publishers, our experience suggests contributors become frantic to be 'rid of' the chapter they have created. It is at this stage where the potential to abuse is at its greatest since few authors 'wish to clap eyes on the darned thing again' (Thompson, 1997) and often pass full control to the editors. Besides the definitional problems involved in talking of power in this context (which we have only alerted readers to in this piece), further consideration of feminist pre-publication practice needs to take place so that the ambivalences, challenges and continuing potentials of feminist editorship can be addressed and built on within women's studies.

Note

1   We would like to thank the book's contributors for participating in the book. They were given the opportunity of commenting on our dialogue. Some of their comments have been incorporated in the final chapter.

References

AISENBERG, N. and HARRINGTON, M. (1988) *Women of Academe: Outsiders in the Sacred Grove*, Amherst: University of Massachusetts.

ATWOOD, M. (1989) 'Sexual bias in reviewing', in DYBIKOWSKI, A. (eds) *The Feminine: Women and Words/Les Femmes et les Mots*, Alberta, Canada: Longspoon, pp. 151–2.

CARTY, L. (1991) 'Black women in academia: A statement from the periphery', in BANNERJI, H., CARTY, L., DELHI, K., HEALD, S. and MCKENNA, K. (eds) *Unsettling Relation: The University as a Site of Feminist Struggles*, Canada: Women's Press.

COTTERILL, P. and LETHERBY, G. (1997) 'Collaborative writing: The pleasures and perils of working together', in ANG-LYGATE, M. and MILLSOM, S.H. (eds) *Desperately Seeking Sisterhood: Still Challenging and Building*, London, Taylor and Francis.

EAGLETON, M. (1996) 'Who's who and where's where: Constructing feminist literary studies', *Feminist Review*, **53**, Summer, pp. 1–23.

GINSBERG, E. and LENNOX, S. (1996) 'Antifeminism in scholarship and publishing', CLARK, V., NELSON GARNER, S., HIGONNET, M. and KATRAK, K.H. (eds) in *Antifeminism in the Academy*, London, Routledge.

GODSELL, M. and MIERS, M. (1994) 'Learning through assignments — A genuine dialogue?', in THORPE, M. and EUNGEON, D. (eds) *Open Learning in the Mainstream*, Harlow: Longman.

HOOKS, B. (1989) *Talking Back: Thinking Feminist, Thinking Black*, Boston: South End Press.

HOOKS, B. (1994) *Teaching to Transgress: Education as the Practice of Freedom*, London: Routledge.

KAPLAN, C. and ROSE, E.C. (1993) 'Strange bedfellows; feminist collaborations', *Signs; Journal of Women in Culture and Society*, **18**, 3, pp. 547–61.

KARACH, A. and ROACH, D. (1992) 'Collaborative writing, consciousness raising, and practical feminist ethics', *Women's Studies International Forum*, **15**, 2, pp. 303–8.

KEITH, L. (1994) (ed.) *Mustn't Grumble: Writing by Disabled Women*, London: The Women's Press.

KITZINGER, C. and WILKINSON, S. (1993) 'Theorizing heterosexuality', in WILKINSON, S. and KITZINGER, C. (eds) *Heterosexuality: A Feminism and Psychology Reader*, London: Sage.

LESLIE, L.A. and SOLLIE, D.L. (1994) 'Why a book on feminist relationship research?', in SOLLIE, D.L. and LESLIE, L.L. (eds) *Gender, Families and Close Relationships: Feminist Research Journeys*, California: Sage.

NGCOBO, L. (ed.) (1988) *Let It Be Told: Essays by Black Women in Britain*, London: Virago.

PEPLAU, L. (1994) 'Men and women in love', in SOLLIE, D.L. and LESLIE, L.A. (eds) *Gender, Families, and Close Relationships: Feminist Research Journeys*, California: Sage.

RAYMOND, J.G. (1993) *Women as Wombs: Reproductive Technologies and the Battle over Women's Freedom*, San Francisco: Harper.

ROBERTS, H. (1981) (ed.) *Doing Feminist Research*, London: Routledge and Kegan Paul.

RUSS, J. (1984) *How to Suppress Women's Writing*, Austin: University of Texas Press.

SKEGGS, B. (1995) 'Introduction', in SKEGGS, B. (ed.) *Feminist Cultural Theory: Process and Production*, Manchester: Manchester University Press, pp. 1–29.

SPENDER, D. (1981) 'The gatekeepers: A feminist critique of academic publishing', in ROBERTS, H. (ed.) *Doing Feminist Research*, London: Routledge and Kegan Paul, pp. 186–202.

SPENDER, D. (1989) *The Writing or the Sex? or Why You Don't Have to Read Women's Writing to Know It's No Good*, New York: Pergamon.

SPENDER, D. and KRAMARAE, C. (1993) (eds) *The Knowledge Explosion: Generations of Feminist Scholarship*, London: Harvester Wheatsheaf.

THOMPSON, S. (1997) Private communication.

WORSLEY, P. (1973) 'The distribution of power in industrial society', in URRY, J. and WAKEFORD, J. (eds) *Power in Britain*, London: Heinemann.

Notes on Contributors

Tina Barnes-Powell

Tina is acting head of department in design management and multi-media at De Montfort University. She is currently writing what she hopes is the final draft of her PhD thesis: 'Young women, power, pleasure and the use of alcohol.' Her research interests include: addictions; young women, the experience of working in higher education; and feminist methodology and epistemology. With reference to hedonistic pleasure, she longs for the day when she has time to fly her 'stunt kite' and attend fully to her mixed borders.

Avril Butler

Avril is a senior lecturer in social work at the University of Plymouth where she has particular responsibility for student placements and practice teaching. She has a master in women's studies and is currently researching in the area of creative autobiography and women's mental health. She is a member of the British Association of Social Workers, the National Organization for Practice Teaching and the Women's Studies (UK) Network. Her other research interests are in feminist social work practice and the sexual harassment of women academics.

Pamela Cotterill

Pamela is a senior lecturer in sociology and women's studies in the School of Social Sciences at Staffordshire University. Her teaching and research interests are in the areas of social policy and social care, feminist epidemiologies and methodologies and relationships between family women. She is the author of *Friendly Relations?: Mothers and Their Daughters-in-law*, and has published articles on feminist perspectives on sociological research, support relationships between family women and humour and social control.

Lena Dominelli

Lena Dominelli holds the Chair in Social and Community Development at the University of Southampton. She has worked as a community worker, probation officer and social worker. She teaches social work and social policy and has written extensively on these subjects. Her most recent key books are: *Anti-racist Social Work*; *Feminist Social Work*; *Women Across Continents: Feminist Comparative Social Policy*; *Gender, Sex Offenders and Probation Practice*; *Anti-racist Probation Practice*; and *Sociology for Social Work*.

LesleyAnne Ezelle

LesleyAnne Ezelle has recently moved to the USA where she is acting as an advocate for sex offenders who also have a learning disability. Prior to moving she was a senior research fellow at Anglia Polytechnic University, focusing her work on staff and service development in the area of sexuality and sexual orientation, specifically as it relates to vulnerable people, as well as those at risk of discrimination. She has written, in collaboration with her colleagues, a number of papers that have explored these issues.

Sally French

Sally originally qualified as a physiotherapist. She then gained academic qualifications in psychology and sociology and, for the past twenty years, has taught social sciences and research methodology to a variety of under-graduate and post-graduate health care students. She worked at the Open University for a number of years and was involved in writing the course *Disabling Society — Enabling Interventions*. She has written and edited a variety of books on disability issues including two on visual disability and one on learning difficulties. Sally French currently works as a part-time lecturer at Brunel University and is also a freelance writer, lecturer, researcher and physiotherapist.

Gabriele Griffin

Gabriele is Professor of women's studies and head of school of cultural studies at Leeds Metropolitan University where she teaches on the Master in feminist studies. From August 1998 she moves to be Professor of English at Kingston University. Her most recent publications include *Gender Issues in Elder Abuse, Feminist Activism in the 1990s, Stirring It: Challenges for Feminism* and *Heavenly Love? Lesbian Images on 20th Century Women's Writing*.

Lindsay Hill

Lindsay is a senior lecturer at Anglia Polytechnic University. She teaches on the diploma in social work and other post qualifying programmes. Her specific area of interest is in child care and child protection. She is currently engaged in an action research project which explores the impact of child abuse investigation procedures on women and children.

Ann Kettle

Ann has taught medieval history since 1964 at the University of St Andrews where she is a senior lecturer. At St Andrews she has held the posts of admissions officer and associate dean of graduate studies in the faculty of arts and of hebdomadar, the officer responsible for student welfare and discipline. Outside St Andrews she has been president of the Association of University Teachers in Scotland (1994–6) and a member of the AUT's national women's committee (1990–4). She chairs the Scottish Higher Education Council's advisory group on its initiative on Women in Science, Engineering and Technology. In June 1996 she was appointed a member of the Scottish Committee of the National (Dearing) Inquiry into Higher Education.

Gayle Letherby

Gayle is a lecturer at Coventry University and teaches sociology and women's studies. She has recently completed her doctoral research which was concerned to explore experiences (predominantly women's) of infertility and involuntary childlessness.

Her other research interests include: the family and kinship; the experience of working in higher education; and feminist methodology and epistemology. With reference to hedonistic pleasure, chocolate and Coronation Street are fairly high on her list.

Danusia Malina

Danusia is a senior lecturer in organisational development and behaviour at the University of Teesside. She has published on academic mothers, cross-cultural research methodology, human resource management and most recently on services marketing issues in women-only sex shops. Her abiding passions are her beloved soldier, their five kids, and her fast car as her chariot of escape.

Sian Maslin-Prothero

Sian is a lecturer in the Postgraduate Division of Nursing at the University of Nottingham. She has written about nursing, social policy and learning. Prior to the world of higher education she had worked as a nurse and midwife in the National Health Service and the Australian outback. Her pleasures are family, gardening, food, wine and laughter.

Carol Munn-Giddings

Carol has a broad background in the social sciences and a masters in Social Policy. Her work experience spans advising on, undertaking and managing research projects in the social services, health and voluntary sectors. She is Director of Research in the School of Community Health and Social Studies, specialising in research related to gender, citizenship and mutual aid community groups. She also lectures in research and evaluative methods to students studying social work and social policy and has a specific interest in the relationship of experience, research, theory and practice. Carol has an eight year old daughter, Ella.

Robyn Thomas

Robyn is a lecturer in organizational behaviour at Glamorgan Business School, University of Glamorgan. Having graduated in Industrial Relationships and Management from University College Cardiff, Robyn worked for several years in accountancy, before taking up a post as a lecturer. Robyn is currently involved in researching the impact of New Public Management on the nature of gendered cultures in universities. In addition, she is involved in a two year ESRC funded project examining new forms of organizational governance in middle management.

Sonia Thompson

Sonia is an African woman of Caribbean descent. Her background is in youth and community work and social work, in England and Jamaica. She is currently working as a full-time lecturer in higher education.

Ruth Waterhouse

Ruth is a senior lecturer in sociology and women's studies at Staffordshire University. Her teaching and research interests are in the areas of counselling, lesbianism and women's humour. She has been involved in women's support groups in Stoke-on-Trent and worked as review co-editor for *Lesbian, Gay, Socialist*.

Sandra Wilkins

Sandra is a senior secretary in the Department of Politics at the University of Southampton. In addition, she is equal opportunities officer for UNISON Southampton Branch and represents clerical staff on various university committees. She has recently completed a Masters degree in equal opportunities studies at Southampton and her dissertation considered the effectiveness of positive action programmes within anti-discrimination legislation in the UK from three different ideological perspectives. She is registered for a PhD.

Index